One-way Ti

C000126847

A Journa

in

Heroic Story of Emily Wilding Davison

First published in Great Britain in 1988

by Bridge Studios,
   4B Bridge Street,
   Morpeth,
   Northumberland,
   NE61 1NB

   Tel: 0670 518101/519561

ISBN 0 9512630 2 1

Cover illustration by James Mayer

Typeset and Printed in Great Britain
by Hindson Print Ltd, Newcastle upon Tyne

(Title page)
The attractive young woman who was Emily Davison. She was said to have lovely
bright eyes which had some special quality, and when she entered a room it lit up.
She possessed a neat figure, but her crowning glory was her thick, golden brown
coloured hair. Emily signed this photograph 'Pem', a strange but intimate
nick-name given to her by school fellows. (Mary Evans – Fawcett Library)

One-way Ticket to Epsom

One-way Ticket to Epsom

by

John Sleight

EXACTLY 75 years ago, on a fine May morning a telegram-boy knocked on the door of the little, grey-stone house in the straggling, rustic Northumberland village of Longhorsley.

The post office message was addressed to the most militant suffragette in England: Emily Wilding Davison.

And in one way or another – in stages of high drama – it was to involve the most famous horse-racing classic in the world; the King and Queen; members of the racing public; the Press from many countries; and the whole of the Suffragette Movement.

The result of the message was the violent death of the 40-year-old woman who received it.

Bridge Studios
Morpeth
Northumberland
1988

John Sleight was for many years Political Editor and a Senior Producer of Tyne Tees Television. As a member of the Parliamentary Press Corps and a Lobby Correspondent he gained an extensive knowledge and insight into the working of Parliament.

Before joining I.T.V. he worked on newspapers in Cornwall and Yorkshire, later moving north to join the editorial staff of the *Evening Chronicle*, Newcastle upon Tyne. Opting for early retirement from Tyne Tees Television in 1985, he was elected Chairman of the Northern Area of the Newspaper Press Fund the following year.

His first book, *WOMEN ON THE MARCH*, published in September, 1986 told the story of seven outstanding women, all of whom became Members of Parliament for the North-East.

John Sleight was educated first at Wakefield Grammar School, then St. Peter's School, York, from where he joined the Royal Air Force to serve five years during World War II.

CONTENTS

Foreword   7

Chapter I   Derby Day Disaster   9

Chapter II   Childhood and Early Influences   22

Chapter III   Emily Joins Up   31

Chapter IV   Emily The Woman   38

Chapter V   The Hell of Emily Davison   48

Chapter VI   Emily and the Northeast Suffragettes   59

Chapter VII   Emily and the Long, Hard Road   71

Chapter VIII   Victory in Death   84

Chapter IX   The Roots and Legend of Emily Davison   102

Bibliography and Acknowledgements   120

ILLUSTRATIONS

	Page
A portrait of Emily Wilding Davison	Title page
The disastrous Derby Day scene of 1913	13
Emily Davison, 'soldier suffragette'	19
The official rosette of the suffragettes	19
Emily, the graduate	29
A suffragette attempts to chain herself to Buckingham Palace railings	33
Suffragettes' attack in Newcastle upon Tyne	37
Old Longhorsley and Corner Shop	39
The torture of force-feeding, as seen by suffragettes	53
Nine suffragettes demonstrate in Newcastle's main street	63
Suffragettes welcomed home at Newcastle Central Station	63
Connie Ellis campaigning on cycle	68
Norah Balls with Emmeline Pankhurst and a group of suffragettes	69
Emmeline Pankhurst in clash with police	76
'The Dashing Suffragette'	83
The mammoth funeral procession in London	85
Enormous crowds in Piccadilly circus watch the funeral	85
The scene at St. George's Church, Bloomsbury after the memorial service	87
Order of Service	88
Emily Davison's coffin arrives at Victoria Station from Epsom	91
The hearse and specially embroidered pall cloth	93
Great crowds at the Morpeth funeral	95
Emily's last resting place, banked high with floral tributes	97
The grave in St. Mary's Churchyard, Morpeth, today	99
Old Longhorsley and Longhorsley today	107
Connie Lewcock (nee Ellis) with the infamous 'Cat and Mouse' poster	115
A last picture of Emily Wilding Davison	117

FOREWORD

Emily Davison is the forgotten heroine of the Suffragette Movement. Her grave on a hill in St. Mary's Churchyard at Morpeth, Northumberland is a rather neglected and untidy monument.

Yet she was the only suffragette to give her life for the great women's campaign to win the vote which was waged for more than 50 years.

The year 1988 is a special year for women and their cause. It is the 60th anniversary of women winning the complete vote; the 70th anniversary of suffrage granted to women of 30; and the 75th anniversary of the death of Emily Wilding Davison. So the time is opportune to tell the heroic story of this remarkable woman.

This book presents telling, new evidence on the manner of her death. For years, people have believed that she went to the Derby to take her own life by throwing herself under the hooves of galloping horses, thus striking a sensational blow for the cause of the suffragettes. The Pankhurst leaders called her a martyr.

New evidence challenges the suicide theory. That evidence is contained in a discovery of Emily Davison's papers and memorabilia called the Rose Lamartine Yates collection. Extensive interviews with old Northumberland suffragette families throw new light on the life and death of Miss Davison – without doubt the most militant member of Emmeline Pankhurst's army of women.

All the world knew about the great drama played out on the Epsom Downs before King George V and Queen Mary. But few people today could tell you much about the life and times of Emily Davison.

What manner of woman was she as she approached the crisis point in her life? At the age of 40 she had achieved the reputation as the most violent campaigner in the whole of the Suffragette Movement, though she always said that she only committed violence because of the violence done to the suffragettes.

Her critics called her a fanatic, a maverick who preferred to take the law into her own hands. An old Northumberland villager called her 'A Wild Lassie'. The Press vilified her, sometimes decribing her as 'Mad Emily Davison'. The older she grew, the more militant she became.

Although the Pankhurst leaders sometimes had to restrain her, they declared publicly their admiration for an outstanding campaigner for the Movement. In apparent contradiction of her violent tactics, Emily Davison was very religious, a regular church-goer who put her Christianity into practice by helping women in need. An innate believer, she seemed to be fired by a practical mysticism. On her most daring exploits, she believed that she was moved by the Will of God.

Over a period of years, she became the scourge of Government Ministers, pursuing them with rare courage and an indomitable spirit, always with the cry, 'Give the vote to women!'

CHAPTER I
DERBY DAY DISASTER
Death of 'The Wild Lassie'

At the end of May in the year, 1913, on the eve of the outbreak of the First World War, Emily Davison was at home in Longhorsley, Northumberland enjoying a rest and recuperating from the rigours of prison life – the price she paid for her militant actions.

The knock on the door of the house with the corner shop where she lived with her mother, Margaret, was from a carrier of a telegram. That message resulted in the most disastrous consequences for Emily Davison, and broke the heart of her mother who loved her dearly. It caused her to pack and leave home within two days; her destination, Epsom Downs.

The legend in the village of Longhorsley is that Emily showed the contents of that telegram to no-one. All that was known was that the 'wire' was from 'The Movement'. Though the late Mr Arthur Wood, of Morpeth, a cousin of Miss Davison's is on record as saying that she discussed some form of demonstration at Epsom with her mother. The exploit was to involve 'a calculated risk' though not a bid for martydom at the feet of galloping race-horses.

What everyone agrees is that after receiving the telegram, Emily Davison 'became rather depressed and was not her usual lively self'. In the carriage of Andrew Jeffreys on the way to Morpeth Station, on her departure, she was distinctly unhappy.

The mystery that remains unsolved is, 'Who sent the telegram?' It certainly did not come from the headquarters of the suffragettes, the Women's Social and Political Union, according to the Pankhursts. It could have come from one of these sources: Miss Davison's own personal cell of London activists; the Epsom cell itself; or from a suffragette group, either in Morpeth or Newcastle.

So what is the most likely source?

On the evidence of the families who knew the Davisons at the time, handed down through their offspring to the present day, the concensus is that the idea sprang from local suffragettes.

One-way Ticket to Epsom

Margaret Oliver, a Longhorsley resident for many years and respected local historian has no doubt. She says that at a meeting of local suffragettes it was agreed that the Derby Day demonstrator would be chosen by the drawing of straws some time before the running of the Derby. Emily Davison drew the short straw. And she was expecting the telegram that would get the mission underway.

Roland Bibby, the Morpeth historian also thinks that the exploit emanated from a local group of suffragettes. And so do many older Northumberland villagers. It is claimed that a group of suffragettes gathered at Morpeth Station to bid goodbye to Emily, who was said to have cried.

When Emily arrived in London, she kept an appointment she did not want to miss as an official of her union, the Women's Social and Political Union; the great four-day Suffragette Summer Festival held in the Empress Rooms, Kensington. In her purse was a four day helper's pass which she took with her to Epsom. She told colleagues she could not attend the next day, she had 'an appointment' but would be back to see them the day after that. When asked to describe her next exploit, all Emily would say was that they could 'read about it in the London evening papers tomorrow'.

Before she left, she paid homage to their patron saint, Joan of Arc, whose large statue dominated one end of the Empress Hall. Emily laid a wreath at her feet, and saluted as a woman soldier should on the eve of battle, for Saint Joan had been her loadstar for many years.

After leaving, she called at the offices of the W.S.P.U. at Lincoln's Inn House and asked for two of the union flags with their distinctive white, green and purple colours.

Asked why she needed them, Emily put her head to one side (a life-time habit) smiled and said nothing. That was the code for some secret demonstration; the union officers gave her the flags and she left. Both were to travel with her to Epsom. That night she stayed with friends in London and prepared herself for the daring task next day.

The English Derby in the early 1900s was a colourful, national festive occasion which attracted enormous crowds to the Epsom Downs, as well as all the fun of the fair. The King and Queen were often present – as indeed they were to see the 1913 Derby. Punters from the East End of London were just as important a part of the sporting canvas as the lords and ladies.

Derby Day Disaster

As the day dawned bright and clear, special horse buses packed with passengers started to leave London for Epsom.

Already, queues of race-goers were forming at Victoria Station to buy tickets for the journey to the course. In the crowd at the station was a middle-aged woman who was dressed to pass unnoticed. She wore a long skirt and large overcoat crowned by a large, dark-coloured bonnet. She walked up to the second-class ticket counter and asked for a return ticket to Epsom. After paying for it, she noticed she had barely five shillings left in her small, black, leather clip-shut purse.

That woman was Emily Davison. She had booked herself on a collision-course which would demand the highest penalty of all. Although she did not know it. In her hand, and rolled up tight and covered to disguise it she carried a union flag. It measured one and a half yards by three quarters of a yard. It was the official Suffragette Flag: white for purity, green for hope and purple for liberty. Hidden inside the back of her coat and pinned securely to the cloth was another rather larger Suffragette Flag. That was her hidden surprise packet. These were her chosen 'weapons' to go into battle for the cause.

Emily arrived at Epsom Downs in good time to see the start of the first race, bought herself an official race-card and made her way to a rise overlooking Tattenham Corner. She perused the runners and riders of the earlier races, and ticked off her fancies in pencil. At last it was mid-afternoon and the time for the big race. There was tremendous tension and anticipation as only the world's most famous horse-race could create. The thoroughbreds – some of the finest horseflesh in the world – lined up at the tape, awaiting Starter's Orders. Suddenly there was a yell: 'They're Off!'

As the runners started to jockey for position in the first few furlongs, Emily Davison's plan was crystal clear. She knew the 'field' would come at a fast gallop round Tattenham Corner and she would have to be quick. The racing thoroughbreds would be bunched together, fighting for supremacy at a key point in the race.

Although her heart was thumping with excitement, her brain was cool and calculating. She knew what she had to do. At first sight of the horses she would rush to the rails, brandishing and flourishing the Suffragette Flag over the course, hoping to cause confusion and disruption. Then step back, the second flag hidden inside her coat held in reserve. There might be a chance in the confusion to display it prominently before the King's very eyes. Even to pin it on his horse. After all, Emily and the Pankhursts had earlier tried to present a petition to the King but had been turned away from the Palace by a show of force.

Suddenly there was the sound of galloping hooves – the leading horses flashed into sight – the rainbow colours of the jockeys' tunics presenting a colourful spectacle. Emily placed her race-card to her eyes, using it as a shield. As the runners came closer, Emily Davison could scarcely believe her eyes. There, running on its own, the King's horse Anmer. What a chance! She would dash under the rails into the middle of the course, straight for the King's horse and rein it down; then remove her hidden colours and pin them on Anmer.

From that moment Emily Wilding Davison was doomed.

That is the picture I have drawn from all the available new evidence and that evidence is strong.

A stills picture sequence of the Derby disaster – printed from the original Gaumont Newsreel Film – shows that at the point of impact the King's horse was clear of all others, both front and rear. Anmer was her only target; Emily can be seen dodging past Agadir in order to reach the Royal mount.

She did not fling herself headlong into the advancing, galloping hooves in a suicide bid – as many people have argued. The pictures clearly show that she had run to the side of Anmer when she made a lunge for his bridle.

It was a plan that went disastrously wrong. Emily Davison was an intelligent woman, but it was naive of her to think that she could halt a powerful thoroughbred in full flight, hurtling towards her at 40 miles an hour – and get away with it.

After the collision the horse stumbled to one side and fell; the jockey, Herbert Jones, was thrown to the ground. Emily was struck by the flying hooves and flung, somersaulting in the air onto the ground some distance away.

Anmer was quickly up. The jockey lay injured, though not seriously, and Emily Davison lay motionless on the turf, now hatless and unconscious, and in the event fatally injured.

Different eyewitness accounts of the accident, reported in many national newspapers next day did not always agree. One of the most accurate and full accounts of the Derby drama appeared in the then *Manchester Guardian*.

This is one eyewitness report in full:

Derby Day Disaster

The unprecedented scene at Epsom when Emily Davison tried to rein down the King's horse, Anmer, and was fatally injured. The distance between Anmer and all other horses indicated Emily could clearly identify it. After stopping the King's horse, her plan was to pin the suffragette flag to the saddle, to publicise sensationally the Women's Cause.

'They had just got round the [Tattenham] Corner and all had passed but the King's horse, when a woman squeezed through the railings and ran out into the course.

'She made straight for Anmer and made a sort of leap for the reins. I think she got hold of them but it is impossible to say. Anyway the horse knocked her over, and then they all came down in a bunch. They were all rolling together on the ground.

'The jockey fell with the horse, and struck the ground with one foot in the stirrup but he rolled free. Those fellows know how to tumble.

'The horse fell on the woman and kicked out furiously, and it was sickening to see his hooves strike her repeatedly.

'It all happened in a flash before we had time to realise it was over. The horse struggled to its feet – I don't think it was hurt – but the jockey and woman lay on the ground. The ambulance men came running up, put them on stretchers and carried them away.

'Most of the jockeys saw nothing of it. They were far ahead. It was a terrible thing.'

That evidence destroys the long held theory that Emily could not have identified the King's horse from a bunch. It also supports my conclusion that she did not dash onto the course to fling herself directly under the horse's hooves.

As though the drama of a suffragette incident was not enough for one Derby day, there were official objections to the result of the race itself. Because the King's horse was at the back of the field it did not interfere with the race leaders.

But there was intense excitement at the winning post as the favourite, Craganour, just held off a strong challenge from an outsider to apparently win by a head. But the stewards received an official complaint about the running of the favourite. The owner and trainer of the beaten outsider claimed their horse, Aboyeur, had been interfered with. The stewards upheld the objection, stating that the favourite was guilty of 'bumping and boring'.

So in another sensation the favourite was disqualified and the outsider became a 100–1 Derby winner! Next day The Times said there had been no Derby racing drama like that for 70 years.

After the race, King George and Queen Mary left in great haste from the back of the grandstand. The Queen, although she sent an aide to enquire about the suffragette's condition, later referred to Emily as this 'horrid woman' at Epsom. The King made enquiries about the jockey. In fact, Herbert Jones had won the Derby for the previous monarch, King Edward, four years earlier.

Emily was rushed to Epsom Cottage Hospital where it was found she had suffered a fractured skull. In was necessary to give her police protection as she was carried from the course for an angry mob, who had lost money on the King's horse, was pressing around.

An operation on Emily afforded some relief, though it could only postpone death by a matter of days. One doctor thought that Emily's thick hair had saved her from instant death. At Epsom hospital, Emily had a number of visitors though she never regained consciousness. Only one member of the family reached her bedside before she died. He was Captain Henry Joycelyn Davison R.N. (Ret.) of Bexhill, a half-brother.

Before Emily died on the afternoon of Sunday, June 8th two very good friends and colleagues from the W.S.P.U., Mary Leigh and Rose Lamartine Yates, entered the hospital and draped the screen round her bed with the suffragette colours. As Emily showed no signs of regaining consciousness, they left. Later that Sunday, Emily Wilding Davison died. There was no one with her when she passed away.

So the most fanatical of all the suffragettes did not live to see women win the vote. Neither was she able to read the last letter from her mother who was not present at the hospital when she died. Was Margaret Davison ill with grief and unable to make the then very long journey from Northumberland to Epsom? Or was there some other reason? Could Mrs Davison have been so shocked by what she called 'a dreadful act' that she could not bring herself to be at Emily's hospital bedside?

Nor did her mother know that another suffragette, Mary Richardson was standing in the crowd at Tattenham Corner on that fateful afternoon at Epsom. It has always been held that Mary Richardson was not party to the plan to cause disruption on Derby Day. I find that hard to accept. She was standing so close to her, she could see she was smiling. And Mary was known to be a good suffragette friend of Emily's. One report said she was Emily's flat-mate. Then there is the newspaper interview with Mary Richardson who said: 'Just before the race started Emily raised some kind of card before her eyes. I was watching her hand, it did not shake. Even when I heard the pounding of the horse's hooves moving closer, I saw she was still smiling. Suddenly she slipped under the rail and ran out into the middle of the course. It was all over so quickly.'

If you talk to the older villagers of Longhorsley today they will tell you a mysterious story of a strong telepathic link between Emily and her mother. When old Andrew Jeffreys went to tell Margaret Davison about the telephone message received by him from Epsom Race Course, she stopped him and said: 'I had a premonition this morning that something tragic was going to happen today. A magpie appeared on my window-sill and would not go away. When I opened the door to go out, the bird flew into the house – I knew it was a bad omen.' That was on Wednesday.

Then on Sunday at 4.50 in the afternoon – the moment Emily died – her mother felt 'something' that went with the flutter of wings through a room in her home. This time she saw no bird. But the last message from her dying daughter had winged its way into the heart of the woman who had borne her.

This spiritual link had existed between mother and daughter throughout their lives. Although Emily once said to her mother 'I never let myself think of you when I do things', Margaret had replied: 'But I often know when you go out on your exploits and danger threatens.'

As Emily lay dying in Epsom Cottage Hospital many enquiries and letters were received from friends and suffragettes. Other letters received were less than loving. Two examples of the hate mail she received are contained in the Rose Lamartine Yates Collection in the Fawcett Library in London.

One dated June 5th, the day after the Derby incident, says:
'I am glad to hear that you are in hospital. I hope you suffer torture until you die. You Idiot.

'I consider you are a person unworthy of existence in this world, considering what you have done.

'I should like the opportunity of starving and beating you to a pulp.

'Why don't your People find an asylum for you?' The outspoken letter-writer was not courageous enough to sign his own name. 'Yours Etc., An Englishman' ends the verbal assault.

The second letter, penned with a black border, equally anonymous and signed 'Yours sincerely, 'A. Roused', dated June 6th, says:
'I as sincerely wish for your recovery as I regret that it is

16

possible. When you are fully conscious it may be that the crazy fanaticism which drove you to break the laws of God and Man will have left your poor brain clearer.

'And in that case surely you will thank Him for sparing you the sin of murder!

'Of course, I cannot hope to touch the heart of a confirmed gaol bird . . .'

There was still much public opposition to the suffragette cause. Her mother's last letter, written in shock and anguish contained perhaps the most surprising tones of all. It suggests the fearsome class gulf between the humble folk of a small Northumbrian village and the ceremonial trappings of a national event attended by royalty. It was a letter that remained unread by the daughter.

The sad letter to Emily read:

'I cannot believe that you could have done such a dreadful act. Even for the Cause which I know you have given up your whole heart and soul to, and it has done so little in return for you . . .

'I know that you would not wilfully give me any unhappiness, and though it must have been some sudden impulse and excitement, I trust you feel assured my earnest and devout prayers will be utmost in your mind.'

If further evidence is needed of Emily's impulsive act on Derby Day there it is in writing from the one closest to her. Her mother talks of 'some sudden impulse and excitement'.

Then there is the evidence of the inquest held at Epsom which found officially that this act was not a suicide attempt: a verdict of 'Death from Misadventure' was brought in.

Mr Gilbert White of Guilford opened the inquest in the new County Court House. The Coroner said that the jockey of the King's horse, Herbert Jones would not be called. A medical certificate said that he was unfit to attend, although he had not been seriously hurt. The first witness called was Captain Henry Davison, Miss Davison's half-brother of Bexhill who knew Emily's work for the suffragettes – but knew nothing about her visit to Epsom.

He said Miss Davison was a B.A. of London University and had taken classical honours at Oxford. 'She was a person of considerable gifts as a speaker and writer'. The Royal Navy Captain said Emily did not go to Epsom with the object of destroying her life. 'She, I think realised the danger, and was willing to accept it, but thought she would be saved'.

Police Sergeant J. Bunn said he was near Miss Davison when she rushed out onto the course. 'I saw the woman throw her hands up in front of the horses. Some had previously passed her.' Police Inspector Whitbread of Stoke Newington said he did not think it possible that Miss Davison could have thought the whole of the horses in the race had passed by, if she had seen some go by. Dr E. Thornley said that the cause of death was a fracture of the skull and haemorrhage of the brain.

The Coroner, in summing up said he thought that Miss Davison's general intention was to upset the race. The jury would probably dismiss from their minds the idea that she intended to take her own life. Emily's mother, Margaret Davison, was represented by the barrister husband of one of her daughter's best friends, Mr Richard Lamartine Yates.

The Metropolitan Police list of Miss Davison's possessions when checked at Epsom Downs were as follows:
Two Suffragette Flags.
One small black leather purse containing three shillings, eight pence and three farthings.
One half return railway ticket, Epsom to Victoria.
One insurance ticket.
Eight half-penny stamps.
One memo book.
One race-card.
One handkerchief.
Envelopes and paper.
One WSPU Helper's Pass.

On examining the purse in London I noticed that through the passage of time, several of the above items had been lost, though the rail return ticket and the insurance ticket are still there.

The story of Emily Wilding Davison was flashed to every corner of the civilised globe. As long as Derby Day 1913 is remembered it will be associated with her name. For she was a pioneer activist who knew no fear.

Many tributes were paid to her: Emmeline Pankhurst, by this time a world-famous figure in the women's movement said: 'We mourn for the loss of a dead comrade, for to mourn is human, but we also rejoice in her splendid heroism.'

Lady Constance Lytton, a greatly respected figure in the fight for votes said: 'I have known her as the most cheerful of companions, the truest upholder of our great cause, and the

Derby Day Disaster

Emily Davison, 'soldier suffragette', awarded the Women's Social and Political Union Scroll and Medal for Valour, after enduring numerous prison sentences for the Cause.

The movement Emily Davison died for. The suffragettes' rosette fashioned in satin ribbon displaying the colours: green for hope, white for purity and purple for liberty.

VOTES
FOR
WOMEN.

most fearless of those who served it.

'Her death is worthy of her life.'

The words of colleague Bertha Ayrton: 'I see that some of our journalists, measuring Miss Davison by their own petty pint-pot standards are calling her mad.

'Mad? Yes! with that divine madness that recreates the world.'

Mrs Edith Mansell-Moullin, wife of the President of the Royal College of Surgeons said: 'She is worthy of the highest rank among the martyrs all down the ages who have voluntarily laid down their lives for a holy cause.'

Her old college companion, Rose Lamartine Yates: 'She had felt the call, she knew that suffering and outraged womanhood looked to her . . . to do her utmost to release them from bondage,'

And from a mere man, Charles Gray who was a much respected figure in the public debate on universal suffrage: 'Emily Davison was one of those who dared calmly to face the "thou art mad" of those who cannot understand; to be ridiculed, ignored and stoned.

'We call those heroes who die for their country on the field of battle; yet it must be far easier to meet death amid all the glamour of an army with banners, than in an hostile crowd bent on holiday.'

One of Miss Davison's intimate friends, Mary Leigh spoke of Emily's 'great gifts', which she devoted whole-heartedly to the Cause.

'She has now been welcomed as a kindred soul by the heroine of old time, the Blessed Joan of Arc'. she said. 'The dauntless heart of Saint Joan still beats in the women of this Movement.'

Once more the name of Emily Wilding Davison was mentioned in the same breath as the French Saint. And the unflinching spirit of Saint Joan must have helped Emily Davison in her agony when she was force-fed no fewer than 49 times, and often brutally handled while serving her numerous prison sentences.

If one sums up the case against claims that Miss Davison committed suicide the evidence is:

She had left friends in London in good spirits, informing them that she would return to the Suffragette Summer Festival the next day.

When she arrived at Victoria Station booking office she bought a return rail ticket back to London.

On the day of her departure from the Longhorsley home, Emily's mother – with whom she had a strong telepathic link – had no inkling that her daughter was going to her death.

Her step-brother, a Captain in the Royal Navy was sure that her death was accidental.

The Coroner found against suicide.

Emily, at this time, was planning further major exploits. She was also writing articles for the Movement and the Press and had an interview for a new post arranged.

Last, but not least, that telling piece of evidence, the union flag fastened inside her coat, to be brought out and pinned to the King's horse after reining it down. That flag was not taken to Epsom without purpose. It was part of a carefully planned operation to be executed on Derby Day.

There the case for Emily Wilding Davison's death by misadventure must rest, so that the saga of an absorbing 40 years of life can begin.

Except to say that the drama from Epsom Downs was to be re-enacted a few weeks later during the running of another horse-racing classic, the Ascot Gold Cup. One Harold Hewitt, a middle aged Londoner and an Old Harrovian, reputedly rather soft in the head, ran on to the course carrying a bible, a revolver and the suffragette flag. He succeeded in stopping the favourite, and brought down the horse and jockey, suffering severe injuries himself.

CHAPTER II
CHILDHOOD AND EARLY INFLUENCES
Rising to the Challenge

Although Emily Wilding Davison was born outside the county, she came from good Northumberland stock – her father from Morpeth, her mother from Longhirst. She was the second child of her father's second marriage.

There is little doubt that Charles Edward Davison, her father, was a major influence in her life. He was an enterprising man with a good business sense. In the Morpeth Parish Register he is described as 'A Gentleman of Independent Means'.

The Davisons hailed as a family from Wooler, Northumberland. Emily's father's great-grandfather, Thomas Davison was appointed Armourer to the Duke of Northumberland in the early 1800s. His son, George, joined him and was so successful he became a Gunsmith with premises in Pilgrim Street in Newcastle-upon-Tyne as well as Alnwick in Northumberland. Charles Edward Davison, who was the second son of George Davison, decided that there was money to be made in Morpeth. He became the owner of a number of private houses there.

He was still a single man; the spirit of adventure stirred within and stories of wealth awaiting in the Dominion of India were enough to tempt him to book a passage abroad. It was while he was setting up business in India that he met the woman he would marry.

Sarah Siton Chisolm, born in Calcutta in 1822 was the daughter of a wealthy family of high rank. Charles and Sarah shared a very fruitful marriage for some years in India, and later in England. In fact Sarah produced nine children in fifteen years. Their first-born, Charles Chisolm Davison, was articled to a Morpeth firm of solicitors when the family returned to England. The Davisons set up home in a large mansion called Winton House in Morpeth which is now the Masonic Hall.

22

Only one child was born there, John Anderson Davison in 1864. All the rest were born in either India or the South of England.

Charles Davison was now attracted to the City of London and he took his family to live in a large house at Blackheath on the outskirts of London. He invested money in a London tramway company.

The family was shattered by the death of their mother, Sarah, when she was only 44 years old in 1866. In need of a mother-figure to bring up his children and run his home Charles Davison met the ideal woman from Northumberland, Margaret Caisley. Some said she became his house-keeper. She is listed in the archives as a 'daughter of a Gentleman'. Her father, John Caisley prospected a drift mine in the coal-rich soil in the countryside around Morpeth.

When Charles asked Margaret to marry him in 1868, he was 45 and she was only 19. By that time the first-born of his first marriage, Charles Chisholm Davison, had been successful as a law student and was planning to set up a lawyer's practice in London.

At any rate, the large family appeared to have got on well together and after Margaret had been married a year, she produced her first child, Alfred Norris Davison. It was three years later, on October 11th, 1872 that Emily Wilding Davison was born at Blackheath.

Her birth brought great joy to both parents. The bond between mother and daughter could not have been stronger. And as Emily developed into a spirited and intelligent child, her father became devoted to her.

Now there was a great band of children in the Blackheath home, though all the children of Charles Edward Davison's first marriage were much older than Emily. The youngest, Isobella Georgina and John Anderson Davison were aged 11 and 8 respectively.

The large Davison family were now in need of a larger house, and while Emily was still a baby they moved to a new home near Sawbridgeworth, a picturesque village on the border of the counties of Essex and Hertfordshire. Gaston House was a large Georgian building with high spacious rooms and a large, pleasant garden. Emily spent many happy years there. It was a joy to play in the nursery and to romp through the lovely gardens.

In living and learning about life during these early years she developed a confidence, not to say a stubbornness. Gertrude Colmore in her book, *The Life of Emily Davison* recalls that Emily would stand on the stairhead by the nursery and defy authority, in the shape of Nurse, to move her.

To shouts of 'come into the nursery and be good', would come the answer, 'I don't want to be good'. Emily did not believe she was being bad but stood there defiantly with arms folded and feet firmly planted, surveying the domestic passing show. That trait remained with her throughout her life. If might was presented as right without good reason, it would be opposed.

Emily was only two years old when a bouncing new baby arrived in the Davison household. Ethel Henrietta was the joy of Emily's life. Emily became 'little mother' and the two little girls were inseparable. They said their prayers together when they were put to bed at night. Often Emily would not go to sleep until mother had allowed them to sing a children's hymn together.

What a busy household Gaston House must have been with a lively band of children bursting with life – to the mortification of servants and governesses! Emily was soon to establish herself as a born leader. When the children wanted sweets, it was Emily who would go in search of mother to ask for, 'Weet, weet' – the closest her little voice could get to 'sweet'. Among the family, 'weet' was to become a nick-name for life. The last postcard that Emily sent her mother from London was signed by that affectionate name.

For six years Emily and Ethel played and laughed together in Gaston House. Suddenly the happiness of the Davison family was broken. Ethel Henrietta, only six, died unexpectedly. It was a cruel blow for that close circle within Gaston House and quite devastating for Emily; the first bombshell to explode in her own small world. The anguish on the face of Ethel's mother was there for all to see. The epitaph on the family grave in Morpeth Churchyard is a reminder of the affection in which Ethel was held. It reads:

IN LOVING MEMORY OF DARLING ETHEL
Died 24th July 1880
Age: Six Years

Emily grieved for her little sister and close companion. But time was the great healer and her religious spirit helped her to forget.

A few years later, Charles Edward Davison decided to move his family into the great metropolis. Settled into her new home, Emily became a pupil at Kensington High School at the age of 13. Emily took with her to Kensington another nick-name, Pem, which sounds rather meaningless. It was a name thrust upon her by earlier playmates as a term of ignominy. Although Pem sounds bland enough, it was intended as a childish term of derision against Emily's stubbornness in absenting herself from a child's version of a military funeral. Emily wanted it her way, with toy soldiers carrying flags and displayed in precise marching columns. Her friends couldn't wait for such correct martial order. When Emily dropped out, they blamed her for spoiling the game. Pem was another life-long name and – purged of contempt – it became her favourite.

Emily as a teenager, was intelligent with a great appetite for learning. Little wonder that she so impressed Miss Hitchcock, headmistress of Kensington High School. At this time Emily was fair-haired, rather pale-looking with bright eyes, and a tendency to hold her head a little to one side as she looked up smiling.

Miss Hitchcock recalled, 'I well remember Emily coming with her father, who was evidently very devoted to her and very much afraid she might be over-worked. She seemed, I remember, delighted to be coming to school and to be with other girls, and that is my impression of her all the time she was there; her pleasure in her work and her interest in everything that went on.'

Emily made good, steady progress at Kensington creating a good impression all round. She was no rebel there; rather a law-abiding girl. As she grew older, her religious tendency increased. There is evidence in two prayer books which Emily carried with her as a pupil. One book contains passages from The Acts. Her stirring interest is shown by words and phrases underlined, and remarked upon in the margin. Sometimes, the modern definition of a word is inserted over the ancient text.

The other, *The Birthday Scriptures Text Book* includes signatures from members of the family, including William Davison, a step-brother. The narrow blue ribbon book-mark identifies the last psalm Emily read: 'In the time of trouble He shall hide me in His Pavilion' (Psalm XXV ii 5) Followed by the verse:

'Hide me O My Saviour Hide
Till the storms of life be past
Safe into the haven guide
Oh, receive my soul at last.'

Too early in Emily's life to be an omen, but readings which show how deeply religious she was, even as a girl. Deborah Jeffreys, of Longhorsley treasures the gift of those two prayer books today. Aside from religion, Emily took a great interest in English literature and the classics. More often than not, her head was in a book. She could be easily moved by a poem. Of the great masters of literature, she adored Shakespeare and Chaucer. She loved to discuss Chaucer's *Knight's Tale* in study with her fellow pupils. Possibly because of her lovely head of golden coloured hair, her friends gave her a new name, 'The Faire Emelye'.

Her Kensington school headmistress wrote of her: 'Emily did not attract as much attention or inspire as many hopes as other more brilliant girls who were her contemporaries. But she had a way of coming out better in examinations than expected, and her essays showed thought and originality above the average.' It would be wrong to think that Emily confined all her interests to learning and the classroom. She had the capacity to cram her life to the full. The evidence is that, had she so wished, she could have made a name for herself in sport. A keen cyclist and skater, she excelled at swimming. After winning a London swimming championship, she was asked to turn professional, but refused. By the time she left school at 19, she was also a very good dancer. Emily also developed a great affection for the London theatre, and attended whenever she could.

When Emily was in her teens, her only full brother Alfred Norris Davison, told her he was considering emigrating to Canada. Finally making up his mind, he left for British Columbia and lived and worked in Vancouver until his early forties, when he died. So Emily was now the only child left of Margaret Davison, though she still had step-brothers and step-sisters.

At this time, Emily's education took a new turn. Paying a visit to a chum at Holloway College in London, Emily very much liked what she saw and was greatly taken with the idea of going to college. After passing the Oxford and Cambridge Higher School Certificate at the age of 19, she went on to win a bursary to Holloway. Another ambition realised, another joy to be part of an excellent centre of learning and to join an old friend!

At Holloway, Emily appears to have been very happy. Her family lived in a nice house in the City of London; her parents were not short of money and she was learning to love all that London had to offer. She studied English literature and mathematics. During those college days, she must have walked past Holloway Prison for Women many times. Little could she have imagined that one day she would be imprisoned within those forbidding walls.

But her happiness at Holloway College came to an abrupt end after only two years. Charles Edward Davison died. He was interred in the family grave in Morpeth churchyard and that sad occasion was to bring Emily to the Parish Church of St Mary's in Morpeth for the first time. Who could know of the cruel stroke of fate that would bring her, also in a coffin from King's Cross, to the same burial ground exactly twenty years later.

After the funeral, Emily wrote a letter to a friend, dated February 15th 1893.
'Mamma has decided that I am to return tomorrow to college. It is very hard to leave them all, but what can one do? Mamma has to pay £20 a term for me, and it must not be wasted. I do not know whether I can stay on after this term, as we do not know how matters are yet, so I must make the best of this term. Mamma is very anxious to keep me at college for my exam if it is possible.'

While Emily felt her father's loss deeply – she was only 21 – she was at first unaware how much his death would change her life. When Probate was granted and details of his estate announced it was found that his fortune had disappeared. One explanation, believed by many people in Longhorsley, is that part of his wealth accrued from his first wife, in India. And that on his death, the monies passed over to the children of the first marriage. Another explanation is that Mr Davison lost money by investment in a London tramway company. A third explanation might be that his wealth declined through a continuous financial drain on his resources.

If one remembers that he had nine children by his first marriage, and three by his second, the financial pressures must have been great, especially as he believed in giving his children a good education. In fact Charles Edward Davison only left about £200, and Margaret's children, including Emily, did not benefit. The result was that Emily Davison had to leave college.

Emily's resilience now showed itself. She was determined to complete the Oxford degree course started at Holloway College, but she needed to earn money at the same time. While her mother, Margaret, had to close up the London home and move to Longhorsley, Northumberland to earn a living, Emily searched for some kind of teaching post. She gained a post as a resident governess, but only with the proviso that she had free time in the evening for private study. She arranged to borrow note-books from college friends who were completing the Honours course in English and thus, in her way, she continued to study for her degree.

The result of that endeavour must have exceeded her wildest dreams: she was awarded a First Class Degree in English Language and Literature. When the Oxford results were announced, Emily was back in Northumberland with her mother, staying in the small house opposite the Shoulder of Mutton Inn in Longhorsley. The house was part of the Corner Shop, where Mrs Davison was making ends meet by baking and selling bread and cakes.

Old Longhorsley villagers still talk about the joy of Emily Davison on receiving the news of her Oxford degree. One villager, Deborah Jeffreys, who married into a family who knew Emily Davison well, put it this way:

'When the news of Emily's success arrived, she ran into her mother's shop, grabbed a jar of black bullets [humbugs] and went looking for the village children. She found them playing on the village green whereupon she opened the jar and flung the contents into the air, much to the children's delight. Emily loved children and wanted to share her delight with them.'

Even an Oxford degree was not enough for Emily Davison. Fired by the achievement of gaining Honours, she now started to read for a London degree. Again she was successful. Well qualified to teach, she decided to accept a teaching post in a London state school. Emily found she had made a mistake. She could not tolerate slow and lazy pupils and their lack of

A woman of learning, literary skill and eloquence. The other side of the extreme militant suffragette called Emily Wilding Davison. Graduated with Honours at London University, and took First Class Honours in English Language and Literature at Oxford.

discipline. So she moved to a private school in Worthing which she found much more congenial. There she was successful in preparing pupils for Cambridge Higher Examinations; it was a most rewarding time.

Later she moved again, this time to take up a post as a private tutor and governess-in-residence. Her happiness in teaching and being with children was easily apparent. She stayed with that southern family for six years. Her teaching career spanned thirteen years, from 1893 to 1906, the year she joined Emmeline Pankhurst and the suffragettes. Over the passing years Emily kept in touch with her college headmistress from Kensington. A firm friendship endured, despite Emily's turbulent years as a militant suffragette; an indication of the loyalty Emily could inspire in others. The old headmistress and her former pupil remained friends to the last.

CHAPTER III
EMILY JOINS UP
The World of the Suffragists

At the age of 33 in the year 1906, Emily Wilding Davison could no longer stand on the sidelines of the great suffragette campaign. Her righteous nature propelled her into the ranks of the woman suffrage soldiers. She had often read in the daily newspapers reports of suffragettes' actions and meetings, which seemed rather biased. In typical Emily fashion, she investigated this doubtful practice for herself.

Emily attended a big meeting and mass rally of the Women's Social and Political Union in London, and heard from the Pankhursts and other leaders direct. Next morning, when she opened the newspapers, there was the confirmation she sought: bias and omission to an alarming degree. When she applied for membership of the Women's Social and Political Union she was accepted immediately and was soon in the thick of things.

After a few, short months the extent of the great challenge ahead was brought home to her with a vengeance. Instead of most of the people supporting their cause, the majority were against. And, instead of one mighty army of women going into battle with the Government, there were two – each following their own strategy and each following independent leaders.

Emily was marching with the more militant union, with Emmeline and Christabel Pankhurst, which had begun in 1903. But there was an even bigger union of women in the field led by an outstanding personality, Millicent Fawcett.

This was called the National Union of Women's Suffrage Societies, which had grown and developed from the small beginnings of a London women's suffrage group, formed as long ago as 1867. Their philosophy was very different to the Pankhurst union. They were constitutionalists and spurned the use of violence. For years, the public had known them as 'suffragists'.

But the arrival of the militant W.S.P.U. caused a change of name. The *Daily Mail*, strongly opposing votes for women, invented the name, 'suffragette'. The newspaper coined that new word because of militant acts and 'unwomanly tactics'. The new name stuck, and the old 'suffragist' name was forgotten.

Emily had only been in the Women's Union for eighteen months when she was appointed an officer of the union, a chief steward. She enjoyed her marshalling duties during the great protest marches through London City. She now had a great fulfilment in her life, working for a cause that superceded all others. She gave up all her teaching duties to become a full-time campaigner.

Moving into a world of confrontation and militant actions, often put down by force of authority, Emily Davison remained an innate believer. A fellow suffragette said of her, 'Emily always said very long prayers and her Bible was always at her bedside'.

During her first two years with the suffragettes, Emily marched and protested with her union without committing any real violent acts. By 1908 the Pankhursts decided that militancy had to be stepped up. It was the only way Government and Ministers would take notice of them and yield. Extreme militancy was the sure road to enfranchisement. So Emily Davison threw herself, with her leaders, into the dramatic, unwomanly act of chaining herself to railings outside Government and other important buildings. Two of her colleagues managed to evade the police, and chained themselves to railings outside 10 Downing Street.

What Emily was quick to discover was that only the Press could awaken the public conscience, and bring about a changed opinion of suffragettes. She started with a flurry to write controversial articles for Fleet Street, though she soon discovered that writing and getting into print were two very different matters. Then she threw in her support behind Christabel Pankhurst, who conjured up the new tactic of disrupting Minister's public meetings. When suffragettes threw awkward questions to Cabinet Ministers, and demanded an answer on the spot, the national Press could not ignore them. Fleet Street was now giving them headlines and much space in its columns.

In March, 1909, Emily Davison was sent to prison for the first time. In a march on Downing Street to present a petition to Prime Minister Asquith, she was arrested and jailed for one month.

A suffragette grapples with police in an attempt to chain herself to the railings of Buckingham Palace. She bears a striking resemblance to Mary Richardson, an extreme militant and friend of Emily Davison. Mary Richardson was at Epsom Downs on June 4th, 1913, the day Emily Davison received fatal injuries during the running of the Derby.

This period was a trying time for Emily Davison and the Pankhursts. Sometime before, the women's campaign as a whole had suffered a stunning blow from a major split. A number of senior figures in the W.S.P.U. were made distinctly uneasy by the autocratic style of leadership by Emmeline Pankhurst and her daughters. The disenchantment spread and a breakaway movement was led by an outstanding woman called Charlotte Despard. Taking a number of experienced colleagues with her, she formed the Women's Freedom League in 1907.

Now the cause for Women's Suffrage was split three ways: the National Union of Women's Suffrage Societies (non violent); The Women's Social and Political Union (militant); and the new Women's Freedom League (militant). Emily stayed loyal to the Pankhursts. But many sympathisers shook their heads at this split in the movement. It obviously played into the Prime Minister's hand to be offered a weakened front. Christobel Pankhurst went as far as to say that had all three different societies united and knocked on the door of 10 Downing Street, their petition could not have been refused. However, it was not to be.

The Pankhursts closed ranks and in July 1909 Emily was in action once more. At a meeting in Limehouse, Lloyd George was the main speaker on the platform. Only two women were allowed in, but a protest against Government policy towards women was actually made by male sympathisers who agreed to argue the women's case. However, directly outside the hall was a group of suffragettes whose shouts and battle-cries caused a distraction. The Police intervened and among those arrested and imprisoned was Emily.

That second sentence of imprisonment for her marked a turning point in the tactics employed by women against the authorities who ran British prisons. It was the decision to begin hunger strikes. The scheming was clever but demanded tremendous courage from the individual woman. Just a few weeks before, a fellow suffragette, Miss Marion Wallace Dunlop had refused food in prison because she was not treated as a Class 1 political offender. The latter offenders had certain privileges, including wearing their own clothes and keeping their possessions. Miss Dunlop was quickly released after she started her hunger strike.

Emily Davison, when informed by the governor that she

would be treated as only a second class prisoner decided that now was the time for a major demonstration within the prison walls. After a struggle she was shut in a cell – and immediately smashed 17 panes of glass. When asked why she had done this she said the cell windows would not open and ventilation was bad. She was facing a two month sentence in prison.

In a letter to a friend dated August 12th 1909 and written from Longhorsley while recuperating, Emily said:

'Then they [wardens] rushed me into another cell in which everything was fixed. I broke seven panes of that window to the matron's utter astonishment as I had a hammer. [How she smuggled this past the prison authorities is not explained].

'Then they forcibly undressed me and left me sitting in a prison chemise. I sang the second verse of 'God Save the King' with 'Confound their Politics' in it! The doctor came to sound me and I refused to be sounded. [Sounding was a medical check on heart and lungs].

'Then I was dressed in prison clothes and taken into one of the worst cells, very dark and with double doors. Then the real grind began. I fasted 124 hours and was then released.'

That numbing torture made her ill and weak, in less than a week she had lost one and a half stones in weight; but her spirit had never been stronger. It was helped by her discovery on a cell wall of a morale-boosting message scratched by a previous occupant; a Mrs Dove-Wilcox had written 'Dum Spiro Spero'. Emily added a line of her own: 'Rebellion against tyrants is obedience to God'. Colmore wrote in 1913 that the key to Emily Davison's *raison d'être* lay in those words written on the walls of Holloway Prison.

During August, Emily was at home in Northumberland with her mother and friends. She loved to walk over the unspoiled moorland countryside, and on a fine day could often be seen reading a book near the banks of the River Coquet. Refreshed and full of vigour to enter the fray once more, she departed for Manchester in September. The capital of Lancashire was a hot-bed of suffragette activity. It was also the home-town of the Pankhurst family. It spawned a number of other outstanding women leaders, not least Annie Kenney, the articulate Lancashire cotton mill girl who wore shawl and clogs.

The Manchester mission was to attend and protest at a budget demonstration at the White City. Five suffragettes smashed panes of glass in the Concert Hall, hurling stones at the glass. All were arrested. Emily, like the rest had the choice of paying a fine or serving two months' imprisonment. They all elected to go to prison so they were committed to Strangeways Gaol where they mutinied and hunger struck. By so doing they were carrying out union tactics. Prompting force-feeding would lead to early release.

The Strangeways prison staff were particularly callous towards the women; the severe treatment included handcuffing them for the first time, and one of them was put into a strait jacket. The jailers failed to break the women and they were released after two days' confinement. Emily then returned to Northumberland.

Early in October, 1909 twelve suffragettes met to discuss plans to disrupt a forthcoming meeting attended by Lloyd George in Newcastle upon Tyne. This is the first recorded incident of violence in which national W.S.P.U. leaders and Tyneside suffragettes combined to stage a major exploit. If all went well, the 'Welsh Wizard' and his entourage would come 'a canny clatter'!

The suffragettes drew up their plans with military precision. Aware that Lloyd George was going to speak to Liberals in Newcastle on Saturday October 9th, they decided to warm up the city population with a big meeting in St. George's Hall on Friday, the night before. Young Liberals heard about the plans and decided to disrupt the suffragettes' meeting, which they did with some effect. In retaliation, four suffragettes smashed windows in the Liberal Club in Pilgrim Street and were arrested.

Fully alerted to the danger threatening Lloyd George, the police tightened up security. Barricades were erected in the Haymarket to allow the Minister safe entry into the Palace Theatre, the venue for the meeting. Despite police vigilance, one daring suffragette broke through the cordon and started to set about the barricade with an axe. She was quickly taken into custody.

As the time for the meeting approached, the suffragettes' plan was triggered. Women slipped into key positions around the theatre, out of sight. Emily Davison and Lady Constance Lytton, a dedicated suffragette and daughter of a former Viceroy of India, were allocated the watch in the lane outside the Newcastle Breweries offices. The women leaders were aware that the Minister might be driven through the back streets.

The situation was tense, a large crowd milled around. An official car, driven by Sir Walter Runciman, safely dropped Lloyd George outside the entrance to the theatre. Then it disappeared into a side street. It suddenly came into sight of Lady Lytton and Emily Davison who rushed forward. Constance Lytton threw a stone towards the car, purposely aiming it below the bonnet to avoid injury to the driver. It hit the front of the car, but before Emily had time to throw her missile, both women were arrested. Wrapped round the first stone was a piece of paper bearing the motto of Emily Davison: 'Rebellion against tyrants is obedience to God'. In court next day, Lady Constance was sentenced to one month's imprisonment, while Emily, much to her annoyance, was discharged.

Drama in the streets of Newcastle upon Tyne. Seconds after this photograph was taken, Lady Constance Lytton (centre) and Emily Davison (hidden behind) attacked a Government Minister's car in the heart of the city. Hidden in a handkerchief in Lady Lytton's left hand is a stone which she hurled at the bonnet of the car driven by Sir Walter Runciman. The suffragettes mistakenly thought the car contained Lloyd George. Emily Davison was arrested.

CHAPTER IV

EMILY THE WOMAN
'Wiles of a Revolutionary'

Emily Davison was 36 years old in 1909 and had been fighting with the suffragette army for three years. She still looked young and attractive with lovely bright eyes, which had some special quality. A friend once said that when Emily entered a room it lit up. She was not very tall, possessed a neat figure but her crowning glory was her golden-brown hair.

Heavily engaged in suffragette exploits as she was, Emily found time for other things. The London theatre was always a great joy to her. Her taste was catholic. She could enjoy a musical comedy as much as a Shakespeare or a Bernard Shaw. A good night out for Emily was to meet up with friends, go to Drury Lane or the Gaiety Theatre and then take supper in the West End. It seems incongruous that a little later on, after inventing the suffragette arson campaign, Emily should help to set fire to a theatre she loved.

She was fascinated by London, it had so much to offer her. A keen interest in the arts often took her to view the latest exhibition of masters at the National Gallery, or catch the latest treasure presented by the British Museum. She adored partying with friends and could be the life and soul of any party, playing the piano and singing with much panache and zest.

Despite all the attractions of the capital city, Emily was only too glad to leave it from time to time to be with her mother in Longhorsley and to recuperate from her exploits, walking in the clear country air of Northumberland. So different from the hurly-burly of city life. Longhorsley itself was a picturesque, straggling little village with pleasing stone houses and two inviting inns, the Rose and Thistle and the Shoulder of Mutton. Quiet but not isolated. Full of canny, shrewd Northumberland country folk. Emily, though not unfriendly, did not mix freely with all the people in the village. Some Longhorsley people said that they never really got to know her. One local family whom she befriended said, 'Emily Davison was pleasant to meet but had an air of reserve, and was uncompromising until she was sure about anyone.'

Emily The Woman

Longhorsley Village in Northumberland as it looked at the time of Emily Davison's death. Emily's stone-built house and her mother's Corner Shop can be glimpsed immediately behind the horse and trap on the left.

Emily is fondly remembered by Winifred Stobbart who no longer lives in Longhorsley. In a letter to a friend some years ago, Mrs Stobbart said that her father, Robert (Bob) Bell sometimes gave Emily a lift to Morpeth in his car. Much to his chagrin, once parked in the middle of Morpeth she would use the open car as a platform to deliver a speech on the need for women's suffrage. Winifred Stobbart vividly recalled the kind of woman Emily was. 'She was a great friend of my parents when my mother was alive and always visited the house when she came to the village', she said. 'Auntie Pem was a favourite aunt. She played the piano well, was very lively, energetic and full of ideas, politically.

'I was quite used to hearing about the Houses of Parliament, and clearly remember her saying to my father, "Bob, if you get a flying machine and take me to the top of the Houses of Parliament I'll blow them up!" My father thought that politically she was quite mad!' Winnie Stobbart loved Auntie Pem. She once said, 'Emily spoke to us with a south country accent and her dentures didn't fit, I liked her'. On her last visit, Emily left a memorial card and a piece of popular sheet music of the day, entitled ironically 'The Policeman's Holiday'.

Eighty years ago in rural counties like Northumberland there was no surging feminist movement as such. The better educated woman might often discuss the theory of universal suffrage. But most of the working class people were fully occupied by the daily toil, the family and the need to earn a living. That is why many country folk found the violent methods used by Emily and her suffragette colleagues unacceptable. Some called her 'The Lawless Lassie', while others said she must be in a state of madness to damage property and to set fire to buildings.

One ageing Northumberland lady said, 'Miss Davison was very intelligent and talented but a fanatic – really two people in one. She could be cool and calm one minute then some impulse would cause her brain to explode like fireworks the next'. Another local lady said, 'A pity that her talents could not have been channelled into something more lasting'. One Northumberland villager said, 'Emily Davison was no heroine in these parts'. Although the same person described Emily's mother, Margaret, as 'a canny body'.

In London, where most of the action was, some of the prominent members of the Women's Social and Political Union had mixed feelings about Emily. One said, 'She is a self-dramatising individualist, insufficiently capable of acting in the confines of official instructions.' Another critic wrote, 'Emily Davison is clever but headstrong. She tends to walk alone.'

During her busy suffragette days, Emily always liked to make time for writing if she could. Her output was prolific with articles for national and local newspapers, as well as letters and pamphlets. Her handwriting reflects her character. The letters are large, bold and clearly written. There is no disputing her passionate and expressive pen which could stir the spirit and spur the doubters on. Sometimes her writings would become rather florid in style, which might explain why Fleet Street editors sometimes rejected her offerings. One editor's letter said that while Emily was not short of talent and original ideas, she would have to tighten up her writing style in order to get published.

In the Rose Lamartine Yates collection in London's Fawcett Library is an album embossed in gold and decorated with reindeer and art-deco lilies. In that, Miss Davison filed cuttings and copies of her many and copious letters to the Press. A glance through the album shows that she spread the word of the Movement around the world.

One of the longest letters in the collection was sent to the

Western Home Monthly in Winnipeg, in which she warns Canadian women not to be side-tracked by scare stories from Britain about their militant actions. She talks about 'Pie-Crust Promises' made by Westminster politicians in the past. Her own newspaper *The Suffragette*, said after Emily's death that her letters to the Press had been written in 'simple lucid terms about the new spirit fast dawning among women of their right to full citizenship'. They might be expected to say that. Whether her style was florid, or not, the passion and sincerity of her letters on behalf of the Cause was always moving.

It is also true that Emily's sincerity and honesty were never in doubt. A minor, but illuminating example of her honesty was evident thumbing through her letters and accounts. Having ordered an item of dress by post from E.D. Soulsby, 29 Bridge Street, Morpeth on April 30th, 1913, Emily spotted that the clothier had forgotten to include postage in his bill, so she added the cost of postage herself. In return Soulsby's wrote to Emily expressing grateful thanks.

Turning to another aspect of Emily Davison's life, one may fairly put the question: 'Did she ever fall in love? If so, with whom?' It seems unlikely that she had no courtship of any kind up to the age of 40 when she died but I can find no trace of a love affair. On the other hand considering her profession, which included years spent as a governess-in-residence, and the total commitment of her last six years to the suffragettes, it is quite possible that she had no time for a man.

Her compensation may have been a number of loyal women friends; apart from Mary Leigh, Rose Lamartine Yates and Mary Richardson, a close companion was described at her funeral as 'Miss Morrison, intimate friend of London'. That is all. However, Miss Morrison remains a mystery figure.

Of all the suffragettes, Emily Davison lambasted Parliament Government Ministers and Prime Ministers more than any other. Lloyd George and Henry Asquith were her *bêtes-noire*. On one occasion, during a visit to Aberdeen she felt sure she recognised David Lloyd George on the main railway station and without further ado attacked 'him' with a dogwhip. 'Lloyd George' turned out to be a local Baptist Minister. The result was another court appearance and this time she was imprisoned for some days. At that time Lloyd George was Chancellor of the Exchequer and had said in Aberdeen that women would already have won the vote but for their extensive militant and violent actions.

But she also waged a war of words, both in public meetings vocally and in letters to the Press. Her ire rose when she perceived Prime Ministers duping her Movement. Henry Asquith, who occupied 10 Downing Street in the explosive years from 1908 to the middle of the First World War came in for some stick. Emily claimed that when Women's Suffrage was debated in public, he side-stepped the issue; but in private he declared himself firmly against votes for women. Records show that Asquith was able to keep Women's Suffrage off the Statute book despite the strong pro-feelings in his own Cabinet. What infuriated the suffragettes was that both Asquith and Lloyd George on the one hand made use of women, and on the other treated them with derision.

A colleague of Emily's, Dr Ethel Smyth, the outstanding composer, said of Asquith: 'I think it disgraceful that millions of women shall be trampled underfoot because of the convictions of an old man who notoriously can't be left alone in a room with a young girl.' That may be an exaggeration but the Prime Minister set aside every Friday afternoon to take a lady friend for a drive. He was of course married.

Lloyd George was willing to place his mistress, Frances Stevenson, as his secretary in 10 Downing Street, but not willing to give her and other women the vote until 1918. Even William Gladstone, in his last term of office as Prime Minister, had done little or nothing in all his years to help women win the vote, yet he could devote many hours during his occupancy of No. 10 on night walks in his personal campaign to save 'fallen women'. Rightly or wrongly, that was Emily Davison's train of thought on the leaders.

Her personal atacks on Westminster also took the form of breaking into Parliament and Whitehall. During 1910, after Asquith promised Parliamentary progress for a Bill for Women's Suffrage and then reneged, Emily smashed windows in the Crown Office. She was fined £5 or a month's imprisonment. She chose the latter but then discovered her fine had been paid without consulting her.

In all, she broke into the House of Commons three times. Her intent was to confront personally Members of Parliament and make a strong protest. But her first attempt was to try and talk directly to Prime Minister Asquith and ask him why, when he was denouncing the action of the House of Lords, he would not make the House of Commons representative by giving votes to women taxpayers? Emily was nothing if not clever and her first break in would take her into Parliament on the Saturday when the Palace of Westminster was quiet, so that she could hide during the weekend and confront Asquith on the Monday morning. Although the attempt failed, it illustrates her strength of purpose and iron will. After the break in she wrote about it in her own words which have been preserved in the archives:

'On Saturday last I entered Old Palace Yard at exactly 2.40 p.m. behind two ladies and went up the stairs into the Royal Gallery, the Princes' Chamber, and the House of Lords.

'When we moved into the Great Central Hall I saw to my joy a little passage out beyond it, and went with the people at right angles to the House of Commons' corridor. There were doors all round it with 'Private' on them. A man passed through one and gave me an idea. As the constable on duty was engaged in conversation, and while the other people were leaving the hall, I tried one of the doors. It gave! I went through. It gave a tiny click, and I was beyond the part which the public were allowed to visit.

'I stood one moment expecting to be seen or stopped, but as no one came I quietly stepped across to a corridor. In the distance through some glass doors I saw a policeman, but luckily he was not looking my way. In the wall I saw a little glass window with a knob, and when I opened it I looked into a dark place which was very hot and found it was the heating apparatus of the Houses. I got in and closed the window.

'There was a series of ladders going up higher and higher into the tower. I climbed up the first with difficulty, as the place was narrow and reached the first platform. I found two fairly firm planks across a pair of rafters, and as it looked dangerous, higher and almost impossible to climb, I took up my abode on one side of this platform and stayed there.

'Then came a period of hideous, awful waiting. The time wore away so slowly, for I had nothing to do but think and read my guide to the Houses of Parliament. I was terribly afraid of being discovered, especially as I had a cold which I could not altogether check with lozenges.

'It was almost overpoweringly hot. The only provisions I had were two bananas and some chocolate. The latter and the lozenges, together with the heat, gradually made me thirsty. I was tired and yet in too uncomfortable a position to sleep. I was also afraid of tumbling over into the well below. Luckily, about 7 o'clock some of the pipes were turned off and I even began to feel cold, so that I put on my jacket again and huddled up.

'The place was indescribably filthy. Years of dirt and dust lay on everything. My face, clothes and head were begrimed. Every now and again with great care I stood up to allay the aching of my bones. 'Big Ben' kept me informed of the slow progress of time, and occasionally I heard the footsteps of some distant watchman.

'At last, about 4 o'clock, morning light began to dawn, and I was truly thankful. Hour by hour passed on, till about 7 o'clock the hot pipes were turned on again. As the day wore on and the heat increased, my sufferings from thirst became so intense that I felt that even if I risked being seized I must descend and look for water. It was the first time that I had left my perch.

'At 1.45 I descended. Arrived at the bottom I opened the glass window cautiously and looked out. No one was about. To my joy I saw just below the window a tap with a little tin dish below it, and 'Cold' printed above it. I climbed out, and as all was silent, eagerly drank some water. It was indescribably comforting. I rubbed some over my begrimed face and hands.

'I dare not stay, so swallowing as much as I could of the blessed water I crept back into the hiding-place and up the shaft. After that I felt capable of waiting on for days, if necessary. I dozed occasionally, and listened for the Abbey afternoon service bells.

'Later on, however, I had to go down again for another drink. Four, five, and six o'clock struck, and once more I felt the need of water. I descended, alas for the last time. I drank of the cool, blessed water eagerly. Then I noticed that as the dish was narrow and flat a good deal of water was spilt on the floor, and fervently hoped no one would pass that way.

'I had just returned to my niche when I heard steps and saw light, for the evening was closing in. I drew back as far as I could, but, of course, the water attracted the watchman's eyes. He opened the door and looked in, and there he saw me.

'What I must have appeared to be I cannot say – a terrible object no doubt. The poor constable was terror-stricken, so that he nearly dropped his lantern. He trembled violently, and called out, "What is it?" He banged the window to, and then he seized his whistle and blew it shrilly. Still trembling, he opened the door again and yelled "Come out!" When I descended he gripped me hard and drew me out of the passage, and there at last appeared another constable, very much astonished.

'After I had washed I was taken quietly to Cannon Row by the station passage, and had a meal which was brought to me by the matron, while they sent in every direction to find a friend who would bail me out, and at last, about 9.30, a constable came in and told me that I was free to go. I could hardly believe it, but found that the authorities had decided not to prosecute me.

'It appears that I could not have been tried in a Police Court, but would have to appear before the House of Commons itself; this is probably the reason I was not prosecuted. I went back to my lodgings to recover cleanliness and ordinary comfort. Such was my visit to the House of Commons!'

On another occasion Emily Davison penetrated the security police on duty at Westminster and was making through Old Palace Yard when she was stopped, arrested and taken to Cannon Row Police Station. She was charged for being within the walls of Westminster for the purpose of committing a breach of the peace. Because the police could not produce evidence of this, Emily was discharged. Her purpose had been 'to address the House of Commons' she informed them.

Emily's third foray into Parliament was linked to the suffragette's rebellion, refusing to take part in the National Census of 1911. The W.S.P.U. case was that as they had no political status what was the point of filling in the papers? Emily declared: 'As I am a woman and women do not count in the State, then I refuse to be counted.'

Her ploy to avoid the census was to absent herself from her home by seeking protection in the House of Commons! On this occasion she successfully entered Westminster without detection; and whether by chance or not she ended up under the shelter of another enemy of Parliament – Guido Fawkes! In fact she spent the night in the Guy Fawkes cupboard. After narrowly escaping the notice of an M.P. showing two visitors round the Palace of Westminster, she found herself in the crypt. But the doors were locked on her and she was eventually discovered by a cleaner. Off to Cannon Row Police Station again but for some unknown reason she was set free after only a few hours spent in the Matron's room. No charge followed.

Looking back on Emily Davison's actions and reactions to

Parliament and politicians, it is obvious that she was unwilling to accept the workings of the democratic system. One can understand the frustration of the Pankhurst group of women after so many years in the wilderness with nothing to show for their campaign, but one cannot evade the question: 'Was Emily Davison – even as a last resort – justified in taking the laws of England into her own hands?'

She caused serious damage to private and public property and even interfered with the safe passage of the Royal Mail. She was the inventor of the national arson campaign, and a leader in the bombing campaign. That must have cost many members of the public much distress.

In attacks on Prime Ministers and others she sweeps to one side the onerous duties of the first Minister of State. Gladstone, for example, during his four terms as Prime Minister had set people free, liberated them from penal taxes and doubled the number of adult males entitled to vote. They were the political priorities of the time, according to the Prime Minister elected by the people. That does not excuse his failure to push forward legislation to give women the vote. It is only in mitigation. Politics is the art of the possible, and the majority of the electors were anti-universal suffrage.

Asquith, entering 10 Downing Street in 1908 soon found himself with a long list of priorities; securing more money from the Treasury to stay ahead in the arms race, maintaining the old age pension, and rallying his forces to push through Parliament health and unemployment insurance. He saw as his first priorities the urgent need to help the poor, the old and the sick. That is not to say that Prime Ministers could be excused. It simply presents another side to the story.

Although he was still struggling with his Parliament Bill in 1911, as well as the Irish Bill, Asquith had continuously ignored Women's Suffrage demands and even warnings from his own Cabinet colleagues. With hindsight, that was a cardinal error. It provoked some of the most violent scenes ever seen involving women in the civilised world; it resulted in some suffragettes being seriously injured and there was considerable damage to property, involving hundreds of thousands of pounds.

Henry Asquith was, eventually, to recognise the worth of women but it was to take the opening salvoes of the first Great War to do it. For, as the men quit their peace-time jobs to put on khaki and leave for the fighting front, the women stepped into their shoes. For their fight was in the munitions factories, on the land, on the buses and in the hospitals.

Among them were the thousands of suffragettes who had withdrawn from their violent suffrage campaign in order to help the country's war effort. But one of their number had already fallen, before the first shot had been fired in anger. She was Emily Wilding Davison. And Henry Herbert Asquith was to leave office in 1916 with nothing to show to help the women's cause. In the end it was to be David Lloyd George's Coalition Government in 1918 that broke the anti-suffrage mould, and for the first time gave the vote to one section of women. However, the woman had to be 30 years old or over and, even then, certain reservations applied! A woman could vote if she lived in her own property, or if a husband owned the property that the wife lived in.

CHAPTER V
THE HELL OF EMILY DAVISON
Victim of Torture

Emily Davison reached new heights of militancy in the last few years of her life – and also suffered the greatest brutality. Only two weeks after the Newcastle upon Tyne incident, Walter Runciman was addressing a large public meeting at Radcliffe, near Manchester. Suffragettes were once more excluded from the hall which prompted a number of women, including Emily, to smash windows in the nearby Liberal Club as a protest.

She was arrested and committed to Strangeways Prison. Emily immediately began a hunger strike. What happened next was Emily's most gruesome experience to date. The day after arriving at Strangeways, she was incarcerated in solitary confinement. That evening two doctors, a matron and five wardresses entered her cell. After a doctor had physically checked her over, he said 'I am going to feed you by force.'

Emily protested that such an operation against her will was illegal. To which the doctor's reply was that it was no concern of his. The senior doctor then grasped Emily by her hair while the wardresses at the same time forced her violently onto the cell bed. 'The scene which followed will haunt me with its horror for the rest of my life,' she said later.

Describing the horror, Emily Davison said: 'While they held me flat the elder doctor tried all round my mouth with a steel gag to find an opening. On the right side of my mouth two teeth are missing; this gap he found, he pushed in the horrid instrument and prised my mouth open to its fullest extent.

'The wardress poured liquid down my throat out of a tin-enamelled cup. What it was I could not say but there was some medicament which was foul to the last degree. As I would not swallow the stuff and jerked it out with my tongue, the doctor pinched my nose and somehow gripped my tongue with the gag. The torture was barbaric.'

When Emily was moved to another cell she found to her surprise that it contained two plank beds, not one. It flashed through her mind that here was a means of barricade. She positioned the beds lengthways between the cell door and the wall of her cell, wedging them tight with a stool and what possessions she had. Then she sat across the beds, adding weight by piling up the table and mattresses on them. That done, she sat tight and waited.

When a wardress returned and tried to open the cell door it would not budge. Looking through the spy-hole she saw why and demanded the door be opened. Emily smiled and said 'No'. After several people had implored Emily to dismantle the barricade a prison superintendent told her 'Get off those planks!' Nothing happened. He then shouted at her 'Davison, if you don't get off those planks we'll turn the hose-pipe on you.' That was a very real threat. No warmth from a summer's day in that prison cell. It was the end of October and now quite cold and dank and a cell without heating.

After smashing a cell window the prison staff pushed through the nozzle of a hose-pipe and pointed it in her general direction. They asked Emily to surrender for the last time. She refused. Then the punishment started. She took the full force of the blast from the hose. 'It was as cold as ice,' she said. 'I had to hold on like grim death. It seemed as if it lasted for an age, that icy flow.'

For about a quarter of an hour they buffeted her with this water cannon. Emily did not surrender. The water was turned off. The warders now decided on force to burst the door open. They warned Emily of the danger of being hurt if the door fell on top of her. But still there was no movement and no reply.

When they burst the door open, warders caught the door before it fell, while another rushed in and seized Emily, shouting the words 'You ought to be horse-whipped for this.'

That was the first time a suffragette had successfully erected a barricade and defied the prison authorities; and the first time the brutality of the water cannon had been inflicted on a suffragette.

Colmore, in her book says that water was six inches deep in the cell. Emily was wrapped in blankets then taken by wardresses to the prison hospital, with women warders speaking of her iron will and determination.

That brutality inflicted on Emily Davison in this northern prison caused a public outcry. Several newspapers demanded an inquiry and at least one called for the removal of those responsible. Crowds gathered outside Strangeways Prison to express their disapproval. The *Manchester Guardian*, as it then was, reported that on one day more than 9,000 people assembled outside the prison to express their concern over her treatment.

Questions were asked in the House of Commons with a strong protest made by Labour leader, Keir Hardie. Philip Snowden, another Labour heavyweight in Parliament suggested that the Prison Visiting Committee, who had sanctioned the use of a hosepipe on the prisoner, should be removed from their offices as JPs.

Even a member of that committee damned the action, stating publicly that as a Justice of the Peace he refused to uphold the action of his colleagues. The Home Secretary had to admit that the JPs had been guilty of a grave error of judgement. Yet, only a few weeks later the same man, Herbert Gladstone, wrote to the authorities at Strangeways commending the medical officer with the words: 'A difficult period has been got through most satisfactorily, owing to the efficiency of the prison service . . . and the good sense shown by the staff'.

The Government was evidently wary about extending too much compassion to the Suffragette Movement, putting the morale of the prison service as first priority. However, Emily Davison was not done yet and in that same month, January 1910, she brought an action against the Visiting Justices of Strangeways Gaol; a major protest against the use of the hose-pipe. Judge Parry, in a reserved judgement found in favour of Emily awarding damages of forty shillings (an amount unlikely to shake the financial foundations of the Visiting Committee), though she did get costs. But the treatment of women in prison seems to have been continued as before and to the best of my knowledge none of the JPs were forced to resign.

Force-feeding of women continued and a particularly graphic account of the torture was given by Emily's friend, Mary Leigh in 'Votes for Women', the official organ of the Women's Social and Political Union.

Imprisoned in Winson Green Gaol in Birmingham after committing a civil disorder, she broke her cell windows in protest. She was removed into an empty punishment cell and handcuffed during the day, except at meals. Mrs Leigh then embarked on a hunger strike. The following account illustrates in painful detail the questionable medical practice of force-feeding.

The Hell of Emily Davison

'The wardresses forced me on the bed with the two doctors who came in with them, and while I was being held down a nasal tube was inserted. It is two yards long with a funnel at one end; there is a glass junction in the middle to see if liquid is passing.

'The end is put up one nostril one day, and the other nostril the next. Great pain is experienced during the process, both mental and physical.

'The sensation is most painful – the drums of the ear seem to be bursting, a horrible pain is in the throat and the breast. The tube is pushed down 20 inches.

'The after-effects are a feeling of faintness, a sense of great pain in the diaphragm or breast bone, though I can't feel it below there. I was very sick on the first occasion after the tube was withdrawn. I have also suffered from bad indigestion.

'I resist and I am overcome by weight of numbers. If the doctor doesn't think the fluid is going down sufficiently swiftly, he pinches my nose with the tube in it and my throat, causing me increased pain.'

The operation was often carried out in an arm chair, specially adapted and placed on a white sheet on the cell floor. It is only when one reads a description like that, that the full horror of force-feeding is driven home. And Emily Wilding Davison was treated to that kind of gruelling experience nearly 50 times in prison!

Soon the Government was to dream up cunning new legislation to try and sap the strength of people like Emily, and to reduce the amount of publicity the hunger strike campaign was getting. The new law soon became known as 'The Cat and Mouse Act', though in Parliamentary papers it was called: 'The Prisoners Temporary Discharge for Ill Health Bill'. It got its name 'Cat and Mouse Act' because it enabled prison authorities to play with sentenced suffragettes as a cat plays with a mouse.

Instead of force-feeding the hunger strikers they allowed the women to continue starvation until their health was endangered; then they were released on licence for a short period, only to have to return to prison on a set date to continue their sentence and if necessary they were re-arrested. In effect, the new law extended a prison sentence to include broken time, and imposed a wearisome, debilitating load on the women falling victims to it.

So the suffragettes struck back and refused to recognise the legislation. Emmeline Pankhurst would have none of it. There was now widespread opposition to the new law and after about six months it was abolished. The suffragettes, in their periods of freedom through the Act had been too much of an embarrassment for the Government.

By 1912 Emily Davison had become a veteran hunger striker with one of the longest prison records, her reward for fighting all out for the Movement. But she was now nearing 40 and the continuous wear and tear on her body through undergoing extended hunger strikes and severe prison conditions was taking its toll. When she was committed to Holloway Gaol in February for launching her arson campaign, she was force-fed immediately. Not because she was on hunger strike, but because her health was so poor. On this occasion she had been sentenced to six months in prison.

After some time, Emily and her imprisoned colleagues once more demanded that they be transferred to the first division in the prison – the division with special privileges accorded to political prisoners. Their demand was refused, so once again Emily decided on drastic action against the prison authorities. Only on this occasion she was to suffer severe injury.

In the Fawcett Library in London is an account by Emily, written in pencil and on yellowing note-paper of what actually took place in June, 1912 when one woman took on the entire prison staff. She felt impelled to make this major protest because her colleagues were being tortured in the same prison. It is such a moving account that I quote it in full:

'On Wednesday, June 19th from 10 a.m. onwards, we were kept in solitary confinement.

'On Saturday morning we decided that most of us would barricade our cells after they had been cleaned out. At ten o'clock on the Saturday a regular siege took place in Holloway. On all sides one heard crowbars, blocks, and wedges being used; men battering on doors with all their might. The barricading was always followed by the sounds of human struggle, suppressed cries of the victims, groans, and other horrible sounds. These sounds came nearer and nearer in my direction.

'My turn came. I fought like a demon at my door, which was forced open with crowbars till at last enough room was made for one of the besiegers to get in. He pulled open the door, and in came wardresses and a doctor. I protested loudly that I

The Hell of Emily Davison

would not be fed by the junior doctor, and tried to dart out into the passage; then I was seized by about five wardresses, bound into the chair, still protesting; and they accomplished their purpose. They threw me on my bed, and at once locked the door and went off to the next victim.

Photograph of an illustration used by suffragettes in their campaign to halt the brutal practice of force-feeding women on hunger strike in prison. Emily Davison suffered this operation no fewer than 49 times. After a team of wardresses pinned the woman down, a doctor pushed a long rubber tube through one nostril and down into the throat, allowing liquid food to enter the stomach.

'I lay like a log for some time. When I did recover a little, I got up and smashed out the remaining panes of my window, then lay down again until I was able to get out into the corridor. In my mind was the thought that some desperate protest must be made to put a stop to the hideous torture which was now being our lot. Therefore, as soon as I got out I climbed on to the railing and threw myself out on to the wire-netting, a distance of between 20 and 30 feet.

'The idea in my mind was "one big tragedy may save many others"; but the netting prevented any severe injury. The wardress in charge ran forward in horror. She tried to get me off the netting and whistled for help. Three others came and tried their best to induce me to go into my cell. I refused.

'After a time their suspicions were allayed, and the matron came through into the ward to visit some of the prisoners; while she was there the wardresses relaxed their watch, and I began to look again. I realised that my best means of carrying out my purpose was the iron staircase. When a good moment came, quite deliberately I walked upstairs and threw myself from the top, as I meant, on to the iron staircase. If I had been successful I should undoubtedly have been killed, as it was a clear drop of 30 to 40 feet. But I caught once more on the edge of the netting.

'A wardress ran to me, expostulating, and called on two of my comrades to try and stop me. As she spoke I realised that there was only one chance left and that was to hurl myself with the greatest force I could summon from the netting on to the staircase, a drop of about 10 feet. I heard someone saying "No surrender!" and threw myself forward on my head with all my might. I know nothing more except a fearful thud on my head.

'When I recovered consciousness, it was to a sense of acute agony. Voices were buzzing around me; in the distance some-one said "Fetch the doctor". Someone tried to move me, and I called out, "Oh don't!" Then the doctor came, and asked for me to be moved to a cell close by. They lifted me as gently as possible, but the agony was intense. It was all I could do to keep from screaming. And then I was placed on the cell bed.

'After a moment the doctor examined me, moving me as little as possible. He asked me to go to hospital, but I begged him to leave me there – which he did. I also managed to say, "For heaven's sake, don't feed me, because I shall fight." I was therefore left very quietly, and they brought me some water, and did all they could for me.

'The first night was one of misery, as I had to lie on my back, although it hurt me to do so. There was no sleep. Next day I at once demanded that the Governor should allow me to have my own doctor to examine me. I said, "If you feed me before examination, it will be at your own risk." The Governor asked me why I had done my deed, and I told him I thought that one big tragedy would save others. His hand trembled, and he promised that he would see into the matter.'

'I was left alone until about two o'clock, when a specialist came in with the prison doctors. He thoroughly examined me, and seemed very much struck with my injuries. Afterwards Dr Sullivan confessed to me that he thought I had had the most extraordinary escape.

'To my amazement the doctors came to forcibly feed me that afternoon. The operation, throughout which I struggled, caused me such agony that I begged the three comrades who were released that afternoon to let friends know outside what was being done.

'From that time on they fed me twice a day, in spite of the torture it caused me, until Thursday, when, to our intense relief, they fed us only once. We all said that any food that could have been poured into us in a second operation could not possibly have done us the good that the relief from a second torture did.

'Meantime nothing was being done to make my condition better. My head was dressed on Sunday. Nothing further was done to it. By the examination I knew that besides the two injuries to my head the seventh cervicle vertebra was injured, and another at the base of the spine. They seemed very much worried about my right shoulder-blade. The sacrum bone was also injured, not to mention the many bruises all over my arms and back. All the vertebrae at the back of the head are very painful, and it is torture to turn.

'On Thursday Dr Sullivan examined me fairly carefully, and asked me to be weighed. I consented and found that I had lost 4 lb. at least since the Friday when I threw myself over. I may mention that when I went into Holloway I weighed 9st. 12½lb., and when released weighed 7st. 8½lb.

'On the Thursday evening after the one forcible feeding operation, the doctor opened my cell door and announced the medical inspector. He walked in and was followed by a

gentleman who gave his name as Dr Craig. The three of them
sat down in my cell and subjected me to a long examination and
cross-examination. I calmly gave them all the information that I
could, and seemed thoroughly to satisfy any doubts they had as
to my sanity.

'In the course of the examination I believe I made them
realise what a disgrace it was to England and the medical
profession that such torture as forcible feeding should have
been resorted to rather than granting justice to women. They
weakly put forward the argument that their only mission was to
save life, but could not deny that mental torture was hardly the
safest way of doing so.

'I also made them realise that we women set this great cause
of ours before everything else in the world; or, as I put it to
them, the cause of human progress was above that of any
possible material consideration.

'Dr Craig thoroughly examined all my injuries, seemed
greatly impressed by them, and when he shook hands with me
said "Don't do any more for your cause; you have done more
than enough."

'On Friday morning Dr Sullivan examined me again, and
told me that I should probably be released that day later on. He
said he would not trouble me with forcible feeding, if when I
was released I would take some food before going out. I said
'Oh no; I absolutely refuse to take any food within the prison
walls'. He therefore decided that he must forcibly feed me
again for the ninth time – which was done.

'All that day I got no chance of letting my comrades know
that I should be released, which they would have been glad of,
because they were all very anxious that I should be. In the
afternoon the doctor came and officially announced my release,
said that all packing must be done for me, and asked me if,
when I was in the cab, I would take some Brand's Essence. He
said that the tin "should not be opened until I was outside, so
that I should know it was not contaminated by the Home
Secretary". I smiled and told him that I was willing to take
anything once I was outside the walls.'

It should be noted that although that moving, hand-written
account, possibly begun in prison and completed when she got
out, was sent to *The Suffragette* newspaper, it was not printed
by them until shortly after her death.

This was probably on the orders of the Pankhursts who

frowned on this sensational incident, and who had been trying to discourage such extreme violent tendencies in Emily.

Looking back over the past 70 years much has been made of this Holloway affair when analysing Emily Davison's character. Some people cited it as evidence of a suicidal tendency which culminated in her death at Epsom.

I must say that I am unconvinced. While admitting courage is a pre-requisite if a leap is going to be made from the railings of a prison corridor to a point below, Emily Davison knew that she was falling onto a wire-netting safety net. On her second leap towards an iron staircase she was once more saved by the corner of the netting clearly in sight. When she made her third fall, it was of a distance of only a few feet from the netting to the floor; and while this was a determined attempt to injure herself, it could hardly be described as a 'death leap' over such a short distance.

Emily says in her account that had she been successful in her attempts she would have undoubtedly have been killed. But she was unsuccessful and made a good recovery from her injuries, though never a complete one. Some of her suffragette colleagues suggested that her attempts in Holloway had been a sensational pretence. I cannot accept that either.

Holloway seems to have been the scene of a climactic act of desperation rather than an all-out attempt at suicide. After all, she personally had been battling for five years without success and was almost certainly the victim of great despondency.

Other retrospective analysts of Emily's character also try to make much of her massive discourse, 'The Price of Liberty' as evidence of her wish for martyrdom. Part of the work contains the words:

'The glorious and inscrutable Spirit of Liberty has but one further penalty within its power, the surrender of life itself. It is the supreme consummation of sacrifice, than which none can be higher.

'To lay down life for friends, that is glorious, selfless, inspiring!

'But to re-enact the tragedy of Calvary for generations yet unborn, that is the last consummate sacrifice of the Militant!

'Nor will she shrink from this Nirvana
She will be faithful "unto this last".'

That verse was unpublished in her life-time and there is no evidence when it was written. The suggestion here is that Emily possessed a vision of a Christ-like sacrifice which would bring about the emancipation and freedom of all women for all time.

It can hardly be said to be a clear, positive statement of intent to commit suicide. It is more like an idyllic dream laced with a touch of fantasy in which the women's cause is linked to stirring Biblical quotations. The verse supports the claim that Emily Davison was a practical mystic who possessed visions of herself as a soldier suffragette, marching forward with the blessing of the Almighty, much in the manner of her life-time heroine, Saint Joan of Arc, who had gone before her.

CHAPTER VI
EMILY AND THE NORTHEAST SUFFRAGETTES
Daring Exploits by Local Women

There is little doubt that the courage and daring exploits of Emily Wilding Davison inspired northern suffragettes who were members of the Women's Social and Political Union. But who was the great inspiration for Emily Davison? Before the dynamic leadership of Emmeline and Christabel Pankhurst, Emily had read of the pioneering work of two northern women who had helped pave the way for the great campaign for votes.

Never showing the same militancy as Emily, those two women impressed through their constitutional skill in helping to prompt the first women's suffrage petition to Parliament in 1866. Emily Davies, daughter of the Revd John Davies of Gateshead was one. Josephine Butler, daughter of Mr and Mrs John Grey, of Dilston, Northumberland was the other.

Emily Davies was also a force in promoting higher education for women and was prominent in the founding of Girton, the first women's college at Cambridge. Josephine Butler fought on two fronts. Aside from the suffrage campaign, she was the leading figure in pressing for the repeal of 'The Contagious Diseases Act'. Under that Act, harsh prostitution laws were invoked. So strongly did Josephine Butler feel about the Act, she later left the suffragists to fight it. She was loath to go, but had no other choice under the suffragists' rules which prevented women campaigning for a second cause.

In June 1866, nearly 1,500 women had signed the Parliamentary petition demanding suffrage. One of the two women chosen to deliver the scroll to Westminster, and to John Stuart Mill, MP, who was to present it, was Emily Davies. The other was Elizabeth Garret of Aldeburgh. Taking the first momentous steps to Parliament, the two women entered Westminster Hall from where the legal business of the nation was conducted in nearby courts. They could see no friendly MP, only a throng of barristers, solicitors and clerks.

Conscious of the message that their petition contained the revolutionary thought that women should also be at work here, they looked around for somewhere to hide their great petition. They saw an old woman selling apples in the corner of the hall, and asked her to hide their papers under her stall, which she did. When the MP arrived to receive them, Emily asked the apple-seller to add her name to the petition!

John Mill successfully presented the petition but little did he know that Britain's women were going to have to wait 60 years before they finally won the right to vote. Still, it was the first, great step in the women's suffrage movement. And it was women like Josephine Butler and Emily Davies who inspired Emily Wilding Davison to become such a passionate fighter for the cause.

While the Northeast region was to produce some of the most militant groups in the country – unsurprising in view of the Emily Davison influence – it was, in the early years rather muted. That is not to say that there were no women working for the cause. There were; but their tactics and strategy were constitutional and within the law. Therefore, without the sensation of violent acts, they were often ignored by the Press. Or, if they were reported, not taken all that seriously.

For instance, when a reception was thrown in Newcastle for Northeast suffragettes returning from taking part in an important London demonstration, the Press treated it as a social occasion. The newspaper reports named the prominent ladies present and described, in some detail, their dresses and adornments!

Extensive public feeling after the turn of the century that women were unfitted for the vote was often reflected in the columns of the local papers.

From the *Morpeth Herald*: 'Such [suffragette] Societies spoil looks as well as manners, for their practices are conducive of self-conceit, forwardness and evil emotions. That is why women who become politicians in early life so seldom marry.'

That kind of remark, from a letter in her local newspaper, made Emily Davison angry. To counteract such outright bias, she often spoke to the electorate in Morpeth, sometimes from an open car in the market-place.

One critic wrote to the *Hexham Courant*: 'The vote has little to do with the unseemly rowdiness and vulgarity of women. It is a sexual unrest, pure and simple, mixed with an idle love of notoriety and vanity. They are unfit to possess power of any sort.'

So, the early campaigners in the north faced formidable obstacles. The starting point for the old 'suffragists' was 1872, when an outstanding character, Mrs Mona Taylor – wife of Thomas Taylor of Chipchase Castle – started to recruit for the Movement. Mona Taylor had a classy and appropriate pedigree – her husband was a wealthy Liberal landowner, and her mother, Elizabeth of Roxburgh, was descended from a well-known, Irish political family.

Mrs Taylor made her first move not long after the first women's petition had been presented to Parliament by John Stuart Mill, MP. She joined the old National Society for Women's Suffrage, and when the much bigger National Union of Women's Suffrage Societies was formed, she became a power in that. Mona Taylor worked hard to spread the word to women that here was something worth fighting for. Elected to the N.U.W.S.S. Executive by leader, Millicent Fawcett, she founded the Newcastle and District Women's Suffrage Society at the turn of the century.

By this time, Emily Davison was watching the activities of the union with interest. Already she was working voluntarily to improve women's role and was naturally drawn to the cause for women's suffrage, though she was disappointed that by following democratic Parliamentary process for some years, the women had made no real progress.

It was that stale-mate that prompted Emmeline Pankhurst, with her daughter, Christabel, to announce the birth of a much more militant group than the N.U.W.S.S. which they called 'The Women's Social and Political Union'. Mrs Pankhurst with her husband, Richard, had worked for the old suffragist movement for some years before that. This militant group, based first in Manchester and then in London, drew Emily Davison to it like a magnet. The fusion of Miss Davison with the Pankhursts was as natural as night following day: here were women of like mind, of indomitable character, courage, intelligence and vision.

Within two years, the Pankhursts had established headquarters in London. With them was another northerner, Annie Kenney, who had worked in a Lancashire cotton mill since the age of 10. Though now she was a bright, attractive, self-educated young woman, who brought many rewarding, working-class ideas into the movement. By 1906, the Pankhursts were stepping up their activities in order to grab newspaper attention. The first suffragettes chained themselves to railings outside 10 Downing Street, while Emily Davison chained herself to railings outside Westminster Abbey. By June 1908, Emily was already at work in London as an Officer of the W.S.P.U. As the Pankhurst Union established a more militant profile than the conformist suffragists led by Emmeline Fawcett, many women started to look towards the Pankhursts for salvation. Women in Newcastle were no exception.

Mona Taylor, still with the Fawcett group of women, thought that Newcastle women could stiffen their opposition to the Government by opposing their candidates in by-elections. However, the N.U.W.S.S. would not have it – so Mrs Taylor and friends split away and formed the first Newcastle Branch of the W.S.P.U.

Under the new colours of white, green and purple, the Suffragette's flag, the calibre of the Newcastle women was soon tested. The hustings opened up with a by-election battle in Newcastle, a three-cornered fight involving Liberal, Unionist and Social Democrat. Emily was fully aware of the importance of this result for, by this time, she was living with her mother at Longhorsley, leaving home from time to time to take part in suffragette exploits in different parts of the country.

It was decided to bring the big guns of the new suffragettes to the Newcastle by-election, but when Emmeline Pankhurst arrived to address a meeting in the Bigg Market she was confronted by a hostile audience. The meeting was abandoned. Other meetings were staged at Trades Union Branches and the County Hotel.

The climax of the campaign, according to David Neville, a local historian, was a demonstration on the Town Moor with Mrs Pankhurst and other front line speakers of the movement. The battle song of the women, was a parody of the 'Keel Row', with the last line revised to: 'Vote for Women and keep the Liberal out!' The women won the day – the Liberal candidate, Edward Short, was defeated by more than 2,000 votes.

Capitalising on the by-election interest, the W.S.P.U. opened an office at 77 Blackett Street, Newcastle, to be run by an experienced national organiser. Mona Taylor and her friends remained active and the establishment of a base in Newcastle was good news for Emily Davison.

Emily and the Northeast Suffragettes

The year is 1912, and for nine years the Pankhursts have been campaigning for votes for women. The Northeast suffragettes, influenced by Emily Davison, were among the most militant in the country. Pictured are nine protesting women marching down Northumberland Street in Newcastle to promote 'The Common Cause'.

A group of Newcastle suffragettes recently released from a southern prison are welcomed home at Newcastle Central Station. The tall woman on the left wearing a sash is Charlotte Marsh, a leading suffragette who carried the Cross at the head of Emily Davison's funeral procession. Note the large Suffragette Flag flying from the carriage of the local leader.

It was not surprising that the next major demonstration in the north should take place in Newcastle involving the Government Minister, David Lloyd George. Emily's part in this exploit has already been written about. Nearly a dozen Newcastle women were sent to prison as a result of this attack, and all of them immediately went on hunger strike, inspired by the record of Emily Davison. Much to her annoyance, Emily was not arrested on that occasion and she left Newcastle for a secret destination to organise another protest against a senior Government minister.

Emily Davison was much in demand to address local suffragette meetings in the Northeast. Stories of her dramatic deeds, to say nothing of grim experiences in prison, captivated audiences. Emily was often impressed by the courage and boldness of the Newcastle suffragettes, as this note to Dr Ethel Williams, one of the local leaders expressed:

'All hail Newcastle, how I wish I were in gaol there!
However, I am busy once more acting as organiser here, ready for a certain person.
I held a first meeting last night. Grand!
The police here are splendid; crowds of children came, they kept them in order and the result was a fine hearing . . . . .

Yours ever in the Cause,
Emily Davison.'

That short note mirrors the exuberance of Emily Davison at this time. She had a great appetite for campaigning, and suicide must have been the last thing on her mind.

Dr Williams, never an extreme militant, fought for the recognition of women in public life for 50 years, was eventually honoured and after her death Newcastle University named a Hall of Residence after her. But in 1907 she had already been a member of the Emmeline Fawcett group of constitutionalists for a year and was strongly enough opposed to the Establishment to march in the 'Mud Procession' through London. The march of women was so called because on a vile, wet Saturday afternoon, police made the suffragettes walk in the gutters! If the Northeast suffragists were split between the Pankhursts and the Fawcetts, there was no enmity between the two factions. Both held their rounds of public meetings, fund-raising events, bazaars and jumble sales. Emily Davison recognised the kudos in maintaining a bond between all like-minded women and when time permitted would accept invitations to speak to any group of suffragettes in the region. A good example of cordial relations between the W.S.P.U. and the N.U.W.S.S. was the formation of a joint choir, which had much success.

By this time there were healthy suffragette branches at Sunderland, South Shields, Jarrow and North Shields, to name but four. Durham County boasted a particularly strong group, including a young militant called Connie Ellis, who was to become a household name in Newcastle as Mrs Connie Lewcock. From a Tynemouth sea-faring family a suffragette named Norah Balls was showing initiative and leadership qualities. She was to become a friend of the Davison family. When Emily Davison invented the new fire-raising tactics in the last year of her life, she was enthusiastically supported by the Misses Ellis and Balls.

Earlier, Miss Balls had been in the thick of militant actions in London streets. She was arrested three times for trying to take a petition to Prime Minister Asquith in the House of Commons. On one occasion, she was accused of assaulting the police who referred to her in court as 'a most dangerous woman'. 'That was always an exaggeration', she said, though she was 'a woman of great spirit'.

Back on Tyneside, she and fellow suffragettes sometimes stood on upturned boxes outside public houses in Scotswood Road, arguing the cause for women's votes. 'There were many lively exchanges outside the pubs!' she once remarked. But the women were never harmed.

By 1912 the Government had decided to crush the suffragettes who now, thoroughly frustrated by Parliamentary delaying tactics, were showing extreme militancy. The Newcastle W.S.P.U. group was no exception and formed part of a mass deputation to the House of Commons. There were ugly scenes when police blocked the route which prompted stone-throwing and window-smashing. The women always amazed the police by their capacity for window-breaking; the secret was that elegant-looking ladies carried hammers inside their fur muffs. Numbers of Northeast women were arrested, though not Emily Davison.

In August of 1912, Tyneside suffragettes severely embarrassed the First Lord of the Admiralty, Winston

Churchill, on a visit to the Tyne. When his boat was delayed at the mouth of the Tyne, quick-thinking Jarrow women hired a boat and, using megaphones, harangued the captive Minister on the river.

In October, 1912, Emily and her colleagues in the W.S.P.U. were shaken by a schism in the movement. The Pankhursts, always rather autocratic, broke away from two key people in the W.S.P.U., a man and wife team who had played leading roles since the early days. Mrs Emmeline Pethwick-Lawrence, Treasurer of the Union for six years, and her husband, Frederick, a brilliant lawyer and fund-raiser for the Pankhursts.

There were also eruptions on Tyneside; the biggest was the resignation of Mona Taylor from the W.S.P.U., objecting to extreme militancy and the new policy of opposing the Labour Party.

It saddened Emily Davison later to see the movement split further when Mrs Taylor founded a new society, calling it 'The National Political League for Women's Suffrage'. Especially as she took several key members with her into the new group. Nevertheless, the militants' campaign had not only to go on but also had to be stepped up. Miss Davison's answer to the Government's refusal to act on votes for women was to invent startling new tactics; fire-raising and bombing!

This period, up to the death of Emily in June 1913, witnessed the most violent actions so far by the women protesters. Emily opened up the arson campaign in London late one morning when she calmly walked up to a Fleet Street Post Office, removed a kerosene-soaked envelope from a container in her bag, ignited it and dropped it into the letter box. As London letters started to burn, she walked on to the nearest Lyons Corner House and took lunch. The Pankhursts and their deputy, Annie Kenney, had no idea what she was up to, but the union soon followed Miss Davison's example and fires, both big and small, started to blaze in different parts of the country.

Early in 1913, the union's 'shock-troops' in Newcastle poured corrosive liquid into several pillar boxes in the city. In addition, suffragettes cut telephone wires at Chester-le-Street. In February, protesting women attacked the Newcastle Labour Exchange smashing windows. Staff picked up a paper message wrapped around an iron bolt which said 'Equal wages for equal work'.

Just days later, the militant women went to Heaton and fired the pavilion in Heaton Park. The Revd Canon Terence Oliver, now of Longhorsley, can recall that blaze. As a boy he was taken to the scene by his father who happened to be the Town Clerk of Newcastle, Sir Arthur Oliver. Attached to the railings, near the pavilion, was a message: 'No peace until women get the vote'.

Two months later Shipcote School in Gateshead was fired. Oil was ignited in the joiner's shop, but it was seen early enough to extinguish before it set fire to the main school buildings.

Although a considerable number of suffragettes in Durham and Northumberland were involved in fire-raising, two women were particularly conspicuous. One of them, Connie Ellis from Esh Winning, who not only knew Emily Davison but was a life-time admirer, was an activist. Joining Emily's Union when she was only 14, she soon learned the skills of a militant, and was only a young woman when she planned her first fire-raising exploits.

She led a party of women who set fire to Esh Winning station. Then an attempt was made to burn down Heaton railway station. And the exploit she loved to recall best, for I was privileged to know Connie, was setting fire to Durham main-line station in North Road. It created a sensation at the time, although the suffragettes failed to inflict serious damage.

'I'm afraid it didn't burn very well,' she said afterwards. 'Though we were always careful not to cause injury to people. I did it to make a militant stand against male supremacy.'

Her most outrageous idea was to blow up Durham Cathedral! She started to plan the exploit in earnest and approached Will Lawther (later Sir William Lawther), the miners' leader, about supplying explosives. 'Will offered to get me the stuff; the idea was to blow up one pier of the Cathedral.' she said. At the eleventh hour she decided to drop the idea. 'I decided against it – I thought I might blow myself up!'

Connie was a teacher when she married a Durham miner and became Mrs Connie Lewcock. She used to say that she was such an active suffragette that her own policeman followed her about, constantly watching over her activities. There couldn't have been many suffragettes with their own private policeman!

Connie Lewcock often fooled the police and, in fact, never went to prison as did some of her colleagues. 'That was my one big, big disappointment in the campaign,' she once said. She also said that Emily Davison's death inspired her to even greater efforts and throughout her life she defended Emily's name against all critics. Connie Lewcock died in 1980.

Connie Lewcock as a young woman, cycling around Durham County to sell *The Suffragette* newspaper and spread the word for Votes for Women. Shortly after this picture was taken, Connie and a colleague were set upon and pelted with stones and clods of earth by a group of angry young men in a Durham pit village.

Norah Balls too, always stood by Emily Davison; she was also a friend of her mother. Before Norah died, she remembered more enjoyable times with the Davisons.

Emily and the Northeast Suffragettes

VOTE AGAINST THE
GOVERNMENT
KEEP THE LIBERAL OUT.

Nº1 Mrs Drummond. Nº2 Mrs Pankhurst.

Historic picture of two suffragette leaders with Northeast suffragettes at a South Shields by-election during the women's suffrage campaign. Emmeline Pankhurst can be seen holding a book. Extreme left is 'General' Flora Drummond, a Pankhurst leader, so called because of her successful military bearing in dealing with awkward authorities. On the extreme right at the rear, behind the lady wearing a headscarf, is Norah Balls, from Tynemouth, who was an outstanding campaigner in the North. She was a friend of Emily Davison.

'Mother Davison, as we used to call her, had a cottage at Longhorsley, and we used to go there on our bikes for a lovely country tea on Sunday afternoons,' she said. Like Connie Lewcock, Norah joined the Suffragette Movement early. She had striking looks and, like Emily, was a woman of indomitable spirit.

As Emily Davison had invented the arson campaign, followers like Norah Balls, put it into practice on Tyneside, often with sensational results. Norah's *coup d'état* was leading a strike force of suffragettes to fire and burn down the stately building, Gosforth Park Hall. It used to stand on a site not far from the present Gosforth Park Hotel. For over 60 years the names of the arsonists were kept a closely-guarded secret. How the secret became known – thereby lies a tale.

Roland Bibby, the Morpeth historian, told me the story.

A few years before she died, Miss Balls, now with an impressive career behind her as a writer, historian, lecturer and magistrate, was asked to address the Annual Dinner of the Association of Electrical Engineers, held in the Gosforth Park Hotel.

69

One-way Ticket to Epsom

The diners were rocked back in their plush seats when they heard Miss Balls say: 'I have not been in this building since 1913, when it was burned down by a group of suffragettes'! Miss Balls did not divulge the names of her other colleagues present that night in Gosforth Park. Another major exploit to help foster the name of Emily Wilding Davison who died that year.

Norah Balls, spending her twilight years in a flat in Bamburgh Castle, lived to see the arrival of a woman in 10 Downing Street. 'A crowning achievement', that met with her approval, she said before she died. She could have easily added; 'It made the suffrage campaign well worth-while.'

The arson campaign spread to other parts of Northumberland. In Morpeth the authorities somehow got wind of the plan to fire the beautiful, 14th century Church of St. Mary's. The Church leaders opened up the old Watch House – used years before when body-snatching was at its height – and posted round-the-clock guards. That was enough to deter would-be arsonists.

Back on Tyneside, another tactic was introduced to disrupt Church Services in Newcastle. But that was to back-fire on the women. When the suffragettes asked to hold an Anniversary Service for Emily Davison, the year following her death, they were refused.

A prominent Newcastle suffragette was Charlotte Marsh. A tall, striking young woman who was involved in numerous exploits and recognised as a good organiser. Known as 'Charlie' to her friends, she was appointed leader of the Nottingham Branch of the Union. She was imprisoned, staged hunger strikes and suffered force-feeding. She was chosen to carry the Standard and the Cross at the head of Emily Davison's funeral. How the outbreak of the Great War changed everything: 'Charlie', purged of her militancy, became chauffeuse to Lloyd George, a Government Minister she had once attacked!

The year 1913 saw the beginning of another explosive campaign by the Newcastle Branch of the W.S.P.U. – bombing! Several bombs were planted in Newcastle, including one in the Newcastle Education Committee offices in the Moot Hall, and, although damage was caused, no-one was hurt. The violence was to continue until the outbreak of World War I.

CHAPTER VII
EMILY AND THE LONG, HARD ROAD
Women's Turbulent Times

It is one of the greatest ironies that the supreme sacrifice made by Emily Wilding Davison – and the continuous struggle by suffragists of all persuasions for over fifty years – did not win them the vote. They had to wait for a World War to do that.

At the turn of the century Emily Davison was 27 and already a woman of accomplishment. She held an Oxford degree, was a teacher and was recognised as a woman with a social conscience. She looked around her at the powerful, rich, British Empire and frowned upon the two different worlds she saw: one wealthy and all powerful, the other poverty-stricken and weak. She made it her business to try and help women in need.

She knew of dockers' families in the East End of London who were on the bread-line. She knew of the widows' struggle to exist on the pittance paid for making Government clothing. She knew of the horrors of the sweat-shop system, under which women worked for less than one shilling per day. She knew that out of every 1,000 babies born, an average of 110 were destined to die within the year because of their mother's pitiable conditions.

She knew that women were exploited, bought and sold in the name of vice, and that even children were outraged and defiled. She also knew that northern women lived in some of the worst slums of the land, that many families existed on bread and potatoes and to some, soup kitchens became a way of life.

Emily Davison could see only one solution. Women would have to help women, and in order to do that, they needed the vote; and then they needed to elect their own Members of Parliament in order to re-define the role of women.

In the year 1900, Victoria was still on the throne. And while the relief of Ladysmith and Mafeking was greeted with rejoicing in London and the capital cities, there was little for women who were suffragettes to rejoice over. Although Emily was still teaching at this time, and not involved in the suffragettes' fight, she was well aware of anti-women feeling.

On the question of Votes for Women, the suffragettes found no ally in the old Queen – in fact she was manifestly against them. Many of her comments on women suffragettes have gone unrecorded, but there are a few gems in the archives. When the Queen heard that a daughter-in-law of a former Prime Minister, Lady Amberley had formed a Suffrage Committee, she was not amused. A letter to the biographer of the Prince Consort, a Mr Theodore Martin, from the Palace said: 'The Queen is most anxious to enlist everyone who can speak or write or join in checking this mad, wicked folly of Women's Rights with all its attendant horrors. Lady Amberley ought to get a good whipping.' On another occasion, the Queen commented: 'The Women's Movement outrages every sense of womanly feeling and propriety.'

The opposition to women's suffrage was widespread from the start and sometimes sprang from the most unlikely sources. When Florence Nightingale was asked to join one of the earliest women's committees she retorted: 'To me, getting the vote is the least of women's problems.' Later, she changed her mind, for she was eventually won over by the women's Cause.

Why was it so difficult for Emily Davison and her comrades to make a break-through? The code of society was to keep women in their place. The last thing the Establishment wanted was to see women in high public office and Parliament. While some mighty men adopted a rather lofty, vapid air about the role of women, others, including Government ministers, were scared of the competition women would provide in Parliament. And they carried out what amounted to an under-cover campaign to block them.

Looking at Emily Davison's life, one has to admire her keen sense of religion and Christianity. She was seen going to church regularly every Sunday when in Longhorsley, and when she was working in London she was never without her Bible. She was devout. Yet, one wonders if she ever thought that the Church itself might have had a role in helping women?

There doesn't seem to be any evidence of the Lords Bishops in Parliament staging a great revolt against the derisory treatment that women received from governments over a period of years, although, a few bishops held a meeting in London in 1913 as a protest against force-feeding. One outspoken sympathiser found his advancement delayed.

Instead, Emily Davison took it out on Government Ministers. Although Emily was dead by the time David Lloyd George was elected Prime Minister in 1916, she lambasted him in the years before that. She wrote many letters to this Government Minister and former Chancellor. Emily's type of militancy was said to be 'the blood relation' of Lloyd George's violent speeches against the extreme militants.

One letter to him, ended with: 'My conviction is that you will never get really good, effective measures for housing, for temperance and social reform, until you get millions of women to co-operate in such legislation. Why don't you counsel women when you bring forward reforming legislation?'

Emily was so frustrated by Lloyd George that on two occasions she thought she would attack him; both failed. On the first, she got the wrong man; on the second, he left a meeting by a side entrance and eluded her.

Emily feared no minister. She was always outspoken against the tactics of Henry Asquith who strung the women along without doing anything.

That did not stop her from directing her fire on a different front. She became a prolific writer of letters to the Press about the unsatisfactory position of women in Britain. In a letter to the Editor of the *Morning Advertiser* she argued for a better deal for the married woman. Reacting to an article which suggested women in marriage should receive equal wages, Miss Davison said that even that was not good enough. The wife who devoted her whole life to the duties of housekeeper and mother had no claim to any part of the husband's means. If she worked with her husband in business, the business was legally his. She had no legal claim to salary or any share of it. He could give it away or sell it. 'The role of the wife in marriage is priceless,' she said. 'But the present position of women in marriage is an anomaly.'

Emily Davison and her colleagues also held strong feelings about women being exlcuded from well-paid occupations. In some cases the Factory Acts operated against women in that they could not work late in the evening. Women were excluded from some professions, including the Bar. They were largely excluded from top positions in the Civil Service. Where they were allowed to compete with men, they were completely outnumbered by male appointments. And, of course, women were not allowed to stand as Parliamentary candidates.

While Emily Davison made use of the letters' column in the newspapers, she was under no illusion about the misrepresentation the women protesters received in the journals of the day. 'The Press stories of militant actions by suffragettes are one of the hardest things we have to fight,' she once said.

Distortions of women's action happened frequently, but one story that Emily told was asking to be mauled by the Press. During the arson campaign, Emily and her friends set fire to a London theatre which resulted in splash headlines emphasising the danger for the theatre-goers. Emily said: 'There was no danger to the public at all, for the attempt was made when the theatre was nearly emptied.' A rather naive comment from the intelligent Emily: did she ever give a thought for the staff remaining in the theatre?

Of the major newspapers of the day, Emily Davison seems to have had the most respect for the *Manchester Guardian*. Even when the *Guardian* condemned violent acts by women, it always opposed the extreme suffering, the force-feeding that women underwent in prison. She once wrote: 'If our nation could only realise the degradation, the unspeakable misery which it involves to the helpless prisoner, it could not allow such re-enactments of mediaeval barbarity to be carried on . . .'

It was not in prison alone that suffragettes were on the receiving end of brutal treatment. They were roughly handled by police on more than one occasion. The worst example of police brutality took place in November 1910 and became known as 'Black Friday' within the women's movement. It involved a march on the House of Commons led by Emmeline Pankhurst, after another Government let-down.

Anger rose in the women after they realised they had been duped by a Prime Minister once again. What happened was that Henry Asquith had been less than luke-warm to women's suffrage until 1910, when the Liberals were returned to power with a much reduced majority. His apparent thinking was that if women were given the vote in the future, the Liberal Party would benefit. So he appeared to offer the olive branch to the belligerent women by hinting that the issue would go to a free vote in the Reform Bill going through Parliament.

When the Bill was given its second reading (main debate) in the Commons in July 1910, Asquith refused to allow time for the stages containing Women's Votes to be added and the important clauses were lost. The Pankhursts, who had called a truce during the hearing of this 'Conciliation Bill', now issued orders for the militant campaign to be resumed.

When Mrs Pankhurst led her troops on a deputation to the House of Commons, they were hemmed in by police in Parliament Square. A gang of toughs, in civilian clothes but thought by the Pankhursts to be employed with the police, waded into the women. In the brutal, pitched battle that followed, women were punched in the face and body, tripped and knocked down. Many were injured and the police then arrested more than 100 of the suffragettes. It was a wonder no-one was killed! Emily escaped unhurt.

In the year 1910, the suffragettes had been employing violence and militant tactics for four years. Was it just a coincidence that the campaign reached its fury when it was joined by Emily Wilding Davison?

The scandalous treatment of women on 'Black Friday' drew protests from many sources. Even the Parliamentary Conciliation Committee demanded that a Public Inquiry be held. But the Government answered 'No', and so the affair died a death. There was an official complaint from the Royal College of Surgeons about the severe injuries inflicted on the women. Charles Mansell-Moullin, Vice-President of the Royal College, said: 'The women were treated with the greatest brutality. They were pushed in all directions and thrown down by the police; their arms were twisted until almost broken. Their thumbs were forcibly bent back and the women were tortured in other, nameless ways. I was there myself and saw many of these things done. It would be interesting to know who issued the instructions that they [the police] were to act with such brutality. And who organised the bands of roughs who suddenly sprung up on all sides from nowhere?'

Despite widespread concern the Government rejected new calls for an inquiry. From this point on, Labour MPs maintained consistent pressure on the Home Secretary and Government to protect the suffragettes from brutality, whether in prison or out. One name that was not uncommon in the House of Commons, was Emily Davison's, especially when MPs were protesting about the continuation of force-feeding. The issue was hotly debated on more than one occasion, but the Home Secretary's attitude didn't change. The operation

One-way Ticket to Epsom

Emily Davison's leader, Emmeline Pankhurst, is here removed bodily by a burly police inspector after a demonstration at the gates of Buckingham Palace. Emily was constantly in confrontation with the police and was jailed numerous times.

would be applied indiscriminately to all hunger-strikers. One MP asked if a model of a force-feeding cell could be exhibited in the Chamber of Horrors at Madam Tussaud's. Another Labour MP, George Lansbury, shook his fist in Asquith's face, declaring that he would go down in history as the man who tortured innocent women.

Although a number of doctors criticised force-feeding, there was no major revolt by doctors as a whole, and numbers of them continued to carry out the operation in prisons. The Pankhursts – and Emily Davison who had been force-fed more times than any other woman – now launched an attack on the medical profession. In a special suffragette pamphlet published from their Kingsway, London Headquarters, they printed the headline: 'DOCTORS AS TORTURERS'. Their message: 'The medical profession has now become a police-force whose task is to break the spirit of the suffragette woman.'

A Dr Hugh Fenton, supporting women, described force-feeding as 'a revolting procedure, and when patients resist, it becomes positively dangerous'. Another doctor said it was intolerable and inhuman to force-feed women.

By 1912 and into 1913, Emily Davison began new tactics – the planting of home-made bombs in public places and official residences. One daring escapade was to smuggle in and plant successfully a home-made bomb in Westminster Abbey. The records show it did not explode. Though another attempt, after Emily's death, was more successful: it blew a piece off the Coronation chair.

But Emily had not done with David Lloyd George yet. Suffragette intelligence sources informed Emily that Lloyd George was in the process of building a large house in Surrey, and that it lay unguarded at night. One night Emily and her accomplices left London by car, discovered the partly-completed home near Walton Heath and planted a bomb which exploded doing serious damage to several rooms. No-one was injured and no-one was caught by the police.

Those incidents were only two of many that Emily and her comrades took part in during the last year of her life, which included attacks on churches, trains and golf-courses. It is surprising how successful they were in their bombing and arson expeditions.

But the suffragettes were amateurs at terrorism. To fire a building, they carried only a small bottle of paraffin, cotton wool, a few shavings and matches. To damage a putting green, they used a small bottle of acid – often to write a suffrage slogan on the hallowed surface!

Naturally, Emily's violent tactics shut her away in prison on numerous occasions in different parts of the country. She was gaoled in London, Manchester, Aberdeen, Birmingham and Liverpool. She served sentences ranging from one month to six months, sometimes suffering the ravages of hard labour. Occasionally, after protesting by hunger strike, she caused the prison authorities to release her after a matter of days.

Emily Davison, at various times, was charged with: demonstrating, causing obstruction, stone-throwing, window-breaking, arson and for assaulting a Baptist Minister. Offences of which she was particularly proud were breaking into the House of Commons on three different occasions.

She was 'inside' so frequently she carried out what amounted to a study of prison life. Her conclusions were that prison was a morally defective atmosphere in which quibble and lies abounded, that the severe enforcement of silence was an incitement to trickery. It taught her to resort to trickery herself to get messages to friends outside. She was a reformist. 'The aim of the future prison system, must be educative and reformative, rather than a deterrent,' she said.

The mental and physical torture demanded heavy penalties of Emily Davison. She once said: 'Every suffragette who puts militancy into practice has to make an enormous sacrifice. It could result in loss of livelihood, position, wealth, friends and relations.' She also added the sacrifice of loss of health, for there is no doubt that her torture in prison plucked away the freshness of her womanhood, making her look older than her 40 years.

In 1912 Emily had served a rather long, gruelling prison sentence. At the beginning of 1913, the year of her death, she had paid the penalty for so much stress and strain. That is evident in a letter she wrote to an old school friend in January of that year. The letter, possibly sent to her greatest school chum, Rose Lamartine Yates, said, after wishing her 'A Happy New Year':

'I was indeed glad to get your card, and to find that you were still willing to "own me"! I had not heard from you for so long that I had almost come to the conclusion that you, like many others, had got to the pitch of thinking I was *too* militant.

Emily and the Long, Hard Road

'I am at present with my mother, who is glad to have me and to know that I am not too battered. The long imprisonment last year, and the terrible finale did not, of course, do me much good but somehow I come up smiling.

'This last four days' hunger strike in Aberdeen, of course, found out my weakness, and I have some rheumatism in my neck and back where I fell on that iron staircase. If it is wet or I am tired both parts ache and I have bumps.

'My mother does not know this thank goodness, and really I look and feel well. At present I have no settled work here or in town. While here I busy myself writing my experiences and doing what I can to help my mother. I wish I could hear of some work though.'

Battered as she was, that indomitable spirit remained within Emily Davison. Was there a yearning for those happy, carefree school days at Kensington? The clue is the signature on the letter, shades of Chaucer, chattering girlish voices and 'The Faire Emelye'. For Emily had signed it with all the affection once shown to her by close companions at school. The signature was, 'Emelye'. Her old nickname.

Living in the more violent days of the suffrage campaign, Emily now saw herself as *the* militant activist of the movement. She wrote, 'As a militant suffragette my time and my energies have been fully occupied in pressing forward my own cause – which is part of the great cause of the people.'

Emily was often questioned about her militancy, threatening injury to many innocent people, the bombing of buildings and the cutting of telegraph wires. She always replied that her cause was also the people's battle. 'Who is the sovereign power but the people?' she would ask. It was very much a case of: 'He who is not for us is against us.'

Nevertheless, some people saw Emily Davison as *the* virago of the suffragettes. That is too simplistic a view. In those turbulent times, she was a kind of warrior. But there was so much more to this woman than that. Her unceasing interest in the Workers' Educational Association; her social work for needy families in London's East End; her appetite for the arts. All are indications of a much broader, appealing and complex character.

One has some sympathy for Emily and her fellow suffragettes. They had campaigned for years, had been patient and trusting at first until driven along more militant paths. It is a sobering thought that the first work in English to challenge the concept of women's inferiority appeared as far back as the end of the 18th century. The book, *Vindication of the Rights of Women* was written by one Mary Wollstonecraft. Then in 1825 a lucid and detailed case for women's suffrage was made in a work by teacher and philosopher, William Thompson.

Both were ahead of their time. It took more than 40 years for the first Parliamentary petition to be presented, a petition that was rejected. The pressure for votes for women then continued to the end of the century and beyond. The suffragettes' campaign took place alongside moves by women to become involved in education, medicine, the law and other professions. Women wanted to make their mark as independent human beings, rather than unequal partners.

The Reform Bill of 1832 did extend suffrage to 'male persons' although complex qualifications applied. But it did nothing for women. The anti-suffragists were in a clear majority. But many people's views of the voting woman were outrageous. A typical comment in the early part of the 20th century: 'Women with the vote would become thinner, sharp featured, lank and dry.'

Some of our great Prime Ministers had to wrestle with the challenging argument of enfranchising women. Taking the first petition to Parliament as a starting point, the issue confronted the Earl of Derby, Benjamin Disraeli, William Gladstone, the Marquis of Salisbury, the Earl of Rosebery, Arthur Balfour, Sir Henry Campbell-Bannerman, Herbert Henry Asquith and David Lloyd George.

Some were more sympathetic to the women's cause than others. All had to weigh women in the balance, with a majority of the electorate opposed. Disraeli was certainly sympathetic to the introduction of women's suffrage, but by 1880 when he left 10 Downing Street for a second time, neither the country nor his colleagues were ready to accept that almost revolutionary change. Campbell-Bannerman was drawn to the women's cause but could not carry his cabinet with him. Balfour was also prepared to accept the women's case, but discovered he could not rely on the support of his Parliamentary colleagues.

While a Conservative Party conference passed a favourable resolution as early as 1887, the Parliamentary leaders were not convinced. Salisbury was then leading the Conservatives. The Liberals, boasting prominent suffragists within their ranks, were equally split. The Labour Party, too, was lukewarm about votes for women. Many Socialists claimed that new legislation extending the vote to women on a property-owning qualification would increase the middle-class vote in the Conservative and Liberal Parties. While a large section of the working class – Labour voters – would remain disfranchised.

One or two of the Labour big guns spoke up for women, politicians like Keir Hardie, Philip Snowden and George Lansbury. But they were too few in number to carry the Party with them. The thorns in the flesh of Emily Davison and the suffragettes were undoubtedly Gladstone and Asquith. Over long periods, they rejected the claims of women. Even when the climate grew more favourable, towards the end of the century and beyond, they would not be moved. Even when the rank and file of the Liberal Party was won over by the women, Asquith was adamant in his opposition.

Lloyd George brought out all the magic of his Welsh political wizardry in dealing with the women's case for votes. In office, he would receive deputations and listen to the suffragette leaders with interest. And it was his coalition Government that passed the first Women's Suffrage Bill in 1918. But he had been ambivalent some years before that. He once told the women leaders that extreme violence by suffragettes had stopped Parliament granting them the vote. In 1912 he opposed the Suffrage Bill before Parliament because it was too limited, giving the vote only to property-owning women. A strange decision to oppose such a momentous step forward on the grounds that it was not generous enough. The 1912 Bill failed.

But violence was not the only tactic tried by the suffragettes. For a time they had outstanding success with a strategy of interrupting Cabinet Ministers speaking at public meetings. That was so sensational then that the Press had to report it. The tactic served to publicise the women's cause, and at the same time made Government Ministers furious!

But the women had a price to pay. Often they found themselves roughly handled at public meetings. The *Daily News* of August 1908:

'It too often happens that the moment a woman raises her voice, even in the politest of questions, she is exposed to violence such as the stewards would never dream of showing to a man for the same cause.'

One-way Ticket to Epsom

One of the worst aspects of the British class-system was seen in the treatment by authority to women of different class. Suffragettes from high society sometimes found that on the same London demonstration they would escape detention, but working class colleagues would not. Similar treatment sometimes applied to force-feeding suffragettes in gaol. While some prison governers were reluctant to force-feed lady suffragettes, ordinary women were force-fed daily without compunction.

That so incensed Lady Constance Lytton, a friend of Emily Davison and probably the leading aristocrat in the Movement, that she decided to provide evidence. Disguising herself as a working woman, on her next arrest by the police she gave her name as Jane Warton. Once inside gaol, after medical examination, she was put through the brutal force-feeding operation without further ado. Previously, as Lady Lytton she had been released almost immediately. There were tragic consequences. Constance Lytton, ill at the time of arrest, suffering from a chronic heart disease, was the victim or irreversible damage to her health. She became a permanent invalid.

It was that kind of prejudice and injustice that fired the spirit within Emily Wilding Davison. She was taken aback by the treatment of her friend, Lady Lytton, whom she had accompanied on previous exploits. Injustice helped to make Emily a rebel. At this stage of her life, in full womanhood, as in earlier childhood, she refused might as right without good reason.

But the Mother of Paliaments was not smiling on Emily and her suffragette fighters yet. Emily Davison was continually perplexed by the entrenched attitude of the British Government especially when other countries were showing the way. How could countries of younger years accord women the vote, when Britain would not?

Australia, New Zealand, Finland and America had already surrendered the vote to women. Even the small island governed by the House of Keys, the Isle of Man, had granted women the vote in 1881. Here in Britain those 'Political Boadiceas' and 'Misguided Women', as they were sometimes called, were going to have to wait and wait for the day of the franchise. But wait or not, every member of that great army of suffragettes was in a fight to the finish!

'The Dashing Suffragette' A contemporary artist's impression of the militant suffragette – rushing forward into action, 'Votes for Women' placard held high, with brolly 'weapon' ready for any eventuality.

CHAPTER VIII

VICTORY IN DEATH

Funeral of Emily Wilding Davison

Emily Davison had taken part in many processions in her militant career – but none like that of her own funeral. Not even her clairvoyance as a practical mystic could have foretold such a triumphal funeral march.

No-one could remember such enormous crowds to witness the last journey of a commoner. It was the greatest tribute ever paid to a woman in Britain. One observer said the pageantry of the funeral recalled the obsequies of Eastern princes. In fact there was a double funeral march, first in London and then in Morpeth.

In the capital more than 5,000 women suffragettes in white, and women supporters in black and purple, marched in columns four deep. And they were followed by hundreds of men who supported their cause. On the funeral route through the capital, more than 50,000 people waited and watched. Every suffragette wore a black arm-band and carried either a Madonna lily, a peony or a purple iris. In the procession were 10 brass-bands and many suffragette banners, worked in white with purple background, the colours of Emily's union.

The leading banner bore the poignant legend that Emily Davison had espoused all her life: 'Fight on and God will give the victory'.

And in the lead position of this moving throng was a tall, handsome, fair-haired woman, Charlotte Marsh, with family roots in Northumberland, who held high the union standard in the form of a gilt Cross. Miss Marsh said afterwards that only the sign of the Cross carved a way through the massive crowds. The march stopped the London traffic.

As the procession made its way to St. George's Church, Bloomsbury, the thousands lining the route stood for the most part, in respectful silence, listening to the bands playing Chopin's 'Funeral March' and the solemn music of Handel. The *Daily Herald* of Monday, June 16th, reporting the events of the day, said the route of the march went through the heart

Victory in Death

Suffragettes in white carrying laurel wreaths form part of one of the biggest funeral processions that London has ever seen. More than 5,000 women were in the procession, which was watched by more than 50,000 people lining the route from Victoria to King's Cross. The banner carries the words of Emily Davison's lifetime motto, 'Fight On and God Will Give the Victory'.

On the day of Emily Davison's funeral, the processional route through central London was so congested that it brought traffic to a standstill. The crowds were enormous everywhere. Piccadilly Circus, seen here, was no exception.

of London's pleasure district. 'There were painted women, sisters of the world's sorrow and vice, who stood on tip-toe to see the coffin of one of their sex who died for them. Their tribute was wonderful.'

Later, one old gentleman in the crowd, pointing to one of the banners, told a reporter: 'They use the sayings of the ancients – dulce et decorum est pro patria mori. (It is a sweet and proper deed to die for one's country) Yet, how few people realise that the woman we have been saluting, died for her country as much as the Indian frontier skirmishers did.' As he spoke, a woman standing near the journalist shouted: 'And the glory of her hair!' Then a message reached the police that a gang of roughs had expressed their intention of smashing up the procession. They must have been overawed by the size and demeanour of the crowd, for they did nothing.

When the procession entered Hart Street a section of the crowd began to boo and hiss. There were cries of 'Three cheers for the King's jockey!' The protests of the rest of the crowd silenced them. In another section of the crowd, pepper was thrown and when a small group of bystanders surged forward in an ugly manner, a contingent of police had to intervene.

Most of the large crowd stood silent and respectful. One old man, his clothes shabby and his shoes worn thin, held a rose in his hand. As the coffin passed he threw the rose on it. 'God bless 'er,' he said.

But the most jarring note to the solemn proceedings of the day was the outrageous action of the police in arresting Emmeline Pankhurst as she left her Westminster flat to join the funeral. The suffragette leader, not fully recovered from a prison sentence, was accompanied by her daughter, Sylvia, and her private nurse. As she left the flat she was straightaway approached by three plain-clothes policemen.

There was a quick exchange of words and then Mrs Pankhurst, visibly shaken, was arrested and taken to Holloway Prison. The Inspector in charge told her she was being returned to prison under the terms of 'The Cat and Mouse Act' (Temporary Discharge for Ill-Health law) under which prisoners on hunger strike and in danger of dying, were released from prison until their health improved when police promptly re-arrested them.

The police were obviously hoping that the absence of the leader would further dampen the spirit of the suffragettes and

Victory in Death

Bare-headed and white-frocked suffragettes with black arm-bands salute the coffin of a dead comrade, as it leaves St. George's Church, Bloomsbury, London, after the funeral service. The furled Suffragette Flag dips in honour of a militant. A strong police presence can be detected to the right of the picture.

supporters but their little plan backfired.

Grace Roe, the chief organiser of the funeral, seizing the initiative, directed the empty Pankhurst open carriage into a key position in the procession. The empty carriage seat holding only the 'ghost' of the leader presented a striking and poignant picture. Even then Mrs Pankhurst cleverly smuggled a note to the marching women urging them to carry on the fight at all costs.

Grace Roe's funeral plans were superbly drawn up, creating a funeral procession that would never be forgotten. Women mourners in purple contrasted with others in white and black. The marching bands were so placed that, as solemn music faded away in one part of the procession it was picked up by another. *The Suffragette* newspaper witnessed the funeral like this: 'To the roll of drums and the muffled chords of Chopin's "Funeral March", the great procession slowly moved forward headed by the Cross-bearer, Miss Charlotte Marsh, her fair hair uncovered. Immediately behind her came twelve white-clad girls with laurel-wreaths and a banner inscribed with Miss Davison's last words: "Fight on and God will give the Victory!"

'This, like all the banners of the W.S.P.U., was in purple worked with silver. Following more girls in white came a dense throng of women in black carrying bunches of purple iris.

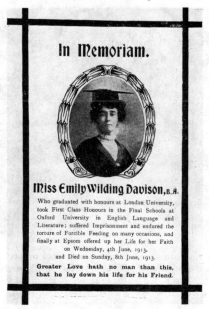

The order of the Memorial Service for Emily Davison. Suffragettes sung her favourite hymns, including 'Fight the Good Fight'. At that service a last tribute on her contribution to the campaign said, 'She worked unceasingly and fearlessly, with all the wonderful ability, literary skill and eloquence she possessed. Finding reason unavailing, she adopted other measures.'

Victory in Death

'They were succeeded by others carrying red peonies, and these, in turn, were followed by a long stream of members in white with Madonna lilies.'

A section of 50 hunger-strikers came next led by the Union Colour-bearer and the banner: 'Thoughts have gone forth whose power can sleep no more. Victory, Victory!' After that came a carriage completely covered with purple and white flowers, then a group of clergy showing their last respects.

Three laurel-wreaths rested on the coffin, placed on an open bier and drawn by four black horses. The silver-edged, purple pall cloth bore two broad arrows embroidered in silver, a tribute to that part of her life imprisoned for the Cause. Walking alongside the four horses and the hearse, were eight suffragettes, among them Sylvia Pankhurst, all dressed in white with black arm-bands. One of the laurel-wreaths from the union bore the words: 'She died for Women'.

Behind the hearse marched a group of women prisoners who, having been charged with conspiracy at the Old Bailey, were out on bail. Following Sylvia Pankhurst and her group was the Chief Mourner, Captain Henry Davison, R.N. (Ret.), a step-brother of Emily's. Miss Davison's university achievements were marked by a large group of women scholars, creating an impressive sight in cap and gown.

Towards the rear, provincial members of the union marched with their London colleagues. Last of all came women from different suffrage societies – as well as men's organisations – all eager to pay a final tribute. One woman was arrested by the police as she tried to pull down a banner at the rear of the procession.

Also in this massive acclamation for Emily Davison were representatives of the Labour Party and the Trades Unions. Ben Tillett walked under the banner of the 'General Labourers' union and 'South London Dockers'.

Christabel Pankhurst, wanted by the police, had to flee to France to avoid a long prison sentence and thus was unable to attend. Annie Kenney was in gaol. The final blow to the leadership was the arrest of the leader that day: evidence of the great crack-down on the Movement by the Police. This long, slow-moving, colourful procession, muted by death though vibrant in life, had a rare pathos and symbolism.

Observers said that the sight of the procession would remain 'An indelible memory'. They could not forget 'the faces of the women and the glory in their eyes.'

The solemn dignity and grandeur of the funeral pageantry could not be spoiled by hordes of detectives who swarmed from one end of the column to the other. Many people in the crowds were neither suffrage supporters nor sympathisers. They were ordinary citizens who could not ignore the suffragette spectacle and such an unusual death. Thousands in the hushed crowds, bared their heads and stood in silence as the hearse passed by. They had never before seen such a manifestation of womanhood.

One journalist wrote: 'They might have been saluting the corpse of some dead conqueror, instead of the dead body of a rebel heroine.' It was, in many respects, the most remarkable funeral that London had ever seen.

The day had begun with the journey of the last remains from Epsom to Victoria Station, London. That was supervised by Captain Davison and attended by Richard Lamartine Yates, a friend of the family. After the funeral proceeded through London to St. George's Church, Bloomsbury, a service was conducted by the Revd C.O. Baumgarten.

According to the newspaper reports, the Chief Mourners were Captain Davison and Mr Yates. Where was Emily's mother, Margaret? Was she too distraught to attend; or was there some other reason? And where were the available, living members of the large Davison family? Was Captain Davison the only one present at the funeral? Perhaps the family of nine had been diminished by death?

After the service the procession moved slowly to King's Cross where the coffin was placed in the carriage of a special train to journey north to Newcastle and Morpeth. On arriving in the station, a large crowd broke through police cordons and barriers, streaming onto the platform to get a glimpse of the coffin. As it was lifted from the hearse, the din of King's Cross traffic appeared to cease and a great silence fell on the throng.

At this touching moment word reached the suffragettes that Mrs Pankhurst had got her message through, despite the close attention of detectives. It read: 'The Government has decided that I may not join with the members and friends in paying a tribute of reverent gratitude to our dear, dead comrade, Emily Davison. I am re-arrested. I return to prison to resume the hunger-strike. I shall do my utmost to uphold the standard of revolt!' So did she.

Emily Davison's coffin arriving at Victoria Station after her death at Epsom. It is covered with a purple pall cloth. A large laurel wreath rests on top of the coffin. Standing sentinel around it are four suffragettes, one of whom is Mary Leigh, another Rose Lamartine Yates, her best friends.

On the main platform the 5.30p.m. train for Newcastle upon Tyne was waiting. The *Morpeth Herald* reported that the body was conveyed in a large brake van, draped with crepe and the colours of the suffragettes' union. Standing guard over the body throughout the journey were six suffragettes led by Mary Leigh, Emily's great friend. They maintained their vigil throughout Saturday night continuing until Sunday noon when the coffin was removed at Morpeth Station. Throughout the vigil one woman held the crepe-draped union flag at the head of the coffin, and another a sheaf of Madonna lilies at the foot.

With bowed heads and statuesque silence they maintained their long vigil, undisturbed by curious passengers who crowded platforms at York, Darlington and Durham, anxious to get a glimpse of the coffin.

There were unforgettable scenes at Morpeth Station on the Sunday when the coffin was removed from the brake-van onto the platform. The suffragette guard stood to attention, saluting on the platform, a moving picture in flowing white dresses and black arm-bands. Each of the women, wearing the official prison badge, now became pall-bearers. It took nearly an hour to remove the numerous floral tributes, totalling more than 200.

In the same train were a large number of suffragettes from as far afield as Glasgow, Dundee, Hull, York, Durham, Newcastle upon Tyne and other northern branches. Some wore tri-colour sashes, the suffragette colours. So many members of the general public wanted to attend the Morpeth funeral that a special train was added from Newcastle.

The hearse was again drawn by four black horses, each with a white leading rope held by a woman in white. It took up a position in the centre of the funeral procession from the station, down the hill *en route* to St. Mary's Parish Church. At its head, the white-robed, distinguished-looking woman bearing aloft a gilded Cross with the Greek monogram 'X.P.'

Next came eight little girls carrying Madonna lilies, followed by members of the Newcastle Branch of the W.S.P.U. They carried a banner, ribboned with the union colours of purple, white and green, bearing the well-known Davison legend: 'Fight on! God will give the Victory'.

The procession, half a mile long, began its slow march amid unprecedented scenes in Morpeth. The whole funeral route, from the station to St. Mary's Field, was lined with a great

The striking presence of white-frocked suffragettes accompany the last journey of Emily Wilding Davison to her resting place in the churchyard of St. Mary's, Morpeth. To the rear, the furled Suffragette Flag, draped in black, dips in salute. Note the silver arrow embroidered on the pall cloth – a recognition of Emily's long, suffering days spent in prison for the Cause.

throng of people, over 20,000 in all.

On cycles, in traps and carriages or on foot, people from all parts of Northumberland, Newcastle and Durham, poured into the town from morning onwards until noon. The local newspaper said that many thousands were attracted by an irresistible curiosity, as well as by sympathy. In the crowd were people from the large mining villages of Ashington, Bedlington and Choppington, and other villages farther off. They also rode in on motor-cycles from as far afield as Bellingham.

The crowd gathered in great numbers outside the railway station where every vantage point was taken. They crowded on the walls on either side of Station Bank, and Mafeking Park was closely packed. People stood six deep on the footpaths, and the Newcastle main road was almost as densely packed.

That Sunday in Morpeth was a glorious summer day with cloudless skies. The long funeral procession was like a religious pageant moving through the streets, the black of the mourners relieved by the white dresses of the suffragettes. And colourful union banners held high. The vast majority of the people showed a sympathetic demeanour as the cortege passed by. Men raised their hats, although a few refused. A small number of anti-suffragists in the town had elected not to draw their house-blinds on this sad day.

At the head of the procession was the Benwell Silver Band, playing first the 'Dead March' and then the 'Marseillaise', the women's marching song. Preceding the coffin were several columns of women in white carrying sheaves of lilies and purple irises. Accompanying them the banner, 'Greater love hath no man than this, that a man lay down his life for his friends.'

Laurel wreaths lay on top of the polished oak coffin which bore this inscription on a brass plate:

EMILY WILDING DAVISON
BORN OCTOBER 11th. 1872
DIED JUNE 8TH. 1913
Fight On! God Will Give the Victory

The responsibility for the funeral arrangements was given to Thomas Smith of Morpeth, in conjunction with the Newcastle officials of the Women's Social and Political Union. He was assisted by William Peters, who later took over the Undertakers which was located for a time in the Herald Office Yard.

The immediate mourners were in five private coaches which followed the coffin. In the first were the Chief Mourners,

Victory in Death

Margaret Davison, Emily's mother and Madame de Baecker, a half-sister from St. Malo, France, and Miss Morrison, who was Miss Davison's intimate companion. The others contained uncles and aunts and cousins. Well-known Morpeth names were there – the Caisleys and the Woods prominent.

Behind the coaches followed local mourners on foot; behind them, a small army of suffragettes, marching in purple and black sections and carrying banners. One banner read: 'I have fought the good fight'. Another: 'To freedom's cause till death'. Following was a draped lorry piled high with wreaths and tributes.

Morpeth, Northumberland, Sunday, June 15th, 1913, the funeral day of Emily Wilding Davison. Down the Great North Road the long procession slowly winds its way to the Parish Church of St. Mary's. A crowd of more than 20,000 people from all over the country lined the route that day. Women's colourful banners were held high in a last tribute to a fallen comrade.

Because of the density of the crowd and the length of the procession, there were several stoppages on the half-mile journey to the churchyard. Forty-five minutes were needed for the cortege to travel from the station to St. Mary's.

When the procession finally arrived at the Parish Church, the band fell back, the banners were furled and stacked and white-robed suffragettes formed a guard of honour up to the beautiful, ivy-covered lich-gate. There is little doubt that when Mr A.R. Fenwick of Netherton built the gate in 1861 he could not have envisaged such a striking procession passing through it.

It was a moving sight as the coffin and white-robed pall bearers, looking like a small pilgrimage, slowly moved up the narrow path to the opening of the lich-gate where the Revd E.R. Wilkinson, senior Curate of St. Mary's was waiting to receive them. Over the well-trod stones of the gate, one or two of the cortege glanced to one side of the inner wall to read the inscription on the stone: 'For the use of the People of Morpeth'. Then they passed alongside venerable gravestones, headstones and ancient masonry, *en route* to the Church.

Many of the people in the procession remained outside while the family mourners and close friends followed the Curate into the ancient Parish Church where the coffin was placed in the chancel. After a brief service, the coffin was borne to the family burial grave located behind the large monument erected in the 14th century in memory of the Revd John Bolland, a Rector of Morpeth.

On rising ground and to the west of the old churchyard with cedar pines standing sentinel, was the Davison burial ground, rounded with three-foot rails on large stone pieces relieved by a central monument of marble bearing a cross.

Emily Wilding Davison was joining her father, Charles Edward Davison, who had died in 1893, and her little sister, 'Darling Ethel' who had died 13 years before her father, aged only six years. At one time it had been rumoured that Emily might have to find another resting place. The local talk was that authorities were apprehensive that the suffragette's grave might turn into a national shrine, causing a disturbance to this secluded corner of Morpeth.

The grave was banked high with floral tributes. Evergreens lined the perimeter of the grave. Some of the tributes had surprising inscriptions. One wreath had the message: 'From a

Emily Davison's grave in St. Mary's Churchyard, Morpeth, pictured shortly after the funeral. In all she received 200 floral tributes from all parts of the country. The ground around the grave was banked high with flowers. Her indomitable spirit was emblazoned in flowers, 'Fight On'.

Gambler's Wife'; another, 'From the heart-broken victim of the man-made marriage laws', and another from 'Two Baby Suffragettes'.

A card attached by white and purple ribbon to a circle of purple and white irises, carried the lines:

'Convict no more, nor shame, nor dole.
Depart – a God enfranchised soul'

One offering was a bunch of pinks in a sun-bonnet trimmed with suffragette-coloured ribbons. Most of the wreaths were from branches of the W.S.P.U. in different parts of the country.

The tribute that really caught the eye was an Aberdeen gift-stone set in the form of an open book on a plinth and made of marble. On the left page was the name of Emily Wilding Davison, on the right page the tribute beginning: 'A veritable Princess of Spirit . . . .' The rest of the inscription has been erased through the ravages of time. The donor has never been identified; the gift-stone carried the message: 'From a loving Aberdeen friend'. One wonders how such a quality carving could have been prepared, inscribed and delivered to Northumberland with such great speed.

Only the members of the family were around the burying place for the committal. There was a touching moment when Emily Davison's final decoration was placed on top of her coffin at the request of her mother. It has been presented to Emily after one of her earlier prison exploits, embroidered on fine, purple cloth, with the words: 'Welcome, Northumbrian hunger striker'.

After the Committal Service many of the suffragettes passed round the open grave and dropped flowers on to the coffin. Many people remained on the scene long after the service was over; while large numbers of people visited the grave, still under its deep layer of flowers, on subsequent days.

There were so many beautiful wreaths from all parts of the country that they presented as rare a spectacle as seen in any churchyard. The wreaths from relatives were testament to their anguish and love. One, in prime place on the grave, had the simple inscription: 'In loving remembrance from her sorrowing mother and sister'. Another was from, 'Captain and Mrs H.J. Davison, with Love and Affectionate Remembrance'. There were numerous tributes from personal friends and sympathisers. One of the largest was from a Baron de Forest. Christabel Pankhurst's final message was: 'With the love and admiration of a comrade'. While her sister Sylvia wrote: 'To honour my dear comrade'. There was a wreath from the Men's Political Union.

Emily Davison's last resting place. The grave on the hill, sheltered by cedar pines and lying to the west of the old churchyard of St. Mary's Parish Church, Morpeth. The inscriptions include the names of her brother, Alfred Norris Davison, who died in Canada, and her sister, Ethel, who died when only six years old.

When I visited the grave early this year I was surprised by the state of the burial place. Time had taken a cruel toll. The iron railing enclosure had vanished, the stone surround had cracked and moved; the central monument with cross presented a greyish appearance and some of the family inscriptions were barely legible.

Strangely, there was no mention on the Davison monument that Emily Wilding Davison was a member of the Suffragette Movement; or that she had died for the cause.

Although a student of political history would seize on words written on the epitaph:

'DEEDS, NOT WORDS'

and,

'GREATER LOVE HATH NO MAN THAN THIS,
THAT A MAN LAY DOWN HIS LIFE FOR HIS FRIENDS'

A further clue might be had in the small, white marble vase standing at the foot of the shrine:
'EMILY WILDING DAVISON'
Died June 8th, 1913.
'VALIANT IN COURAGE AND FAITH'
The grave was not easy to find. There are no directions of any kind.

For many years her close friend, Mary Leigh sent a wreath of flowers on the anniversary of her death. Occasionally other flowers have appeared on the grave but in recent years their numbers have dwindled.

When Emily's mortal remains were lowered into the burial ground 75 years ago the grave had been banked high with floral tributes from all over England.

Since my visit to the grave in early January, Morpeth town has decided that this year's 75th anniversary of Emily Davison's death deserves special recognition. The militant suffragette may have had to wait several decades to be acclaimed by the Town Fathers, but is welcome for all that. And Morpeth is not alone in recognising the importance of Miss Davison this year. Government, once so strongly opposed to her, has now singled out her grave for special protection. Her grave is one of several features in Morpeth churchyard selected for listing in a survey by the Department of the Environment.

Victory in Death

Castle Morpeth Borough council is drawing up plans to re-instate and tidy up the Davison burial ground in St. Mary's churchyard. The scheme includes replacement of the iron railing enclosures, repairing of the cracked stone surround, and re-lettering of the family epitaphs. There is also another idea, supported by Morpeth Parish Council, to erect a plaque in Emily Davison's memory in Longhorsley.

One woman who walked past the open grave all those years ago to pay her final tribute, tossing a purple iris on to the coffin was Connie Lewcock, a lifetime admirer of Emily's. Recalling the day of the funeral some years ago, she said:

'It was a lovely sunny day and I travelled from Durham to be there. Hundreds of men and women turned out, many weeping openly . . . . it was one of the biggest days Morpeth has ever seen.'

CHAPTER IX
THE ROOTS AND LEGEND OF EMILY DAVISON
Decorated for Valour

Since her violent death the name of Emily Davison has become legendary. But the legend has dimmed with the passing of time. What do the many thousands of today's women voters remember about Emily, other than the story of her fatal attempt to stop the King's horse in the Derby. Very little has been written about her these past seventy-five years. Though she was the only suffragette 'killed in action' and the Pankhurst leaders called her a martyr. She was also the unofficial leader of the most militant suffragettes.

Attempts have been made to remember and revere the name of this famous, north-country woman. One close friend did set up a kind of women's club during the First World War to perpetuate her memory, though there is no record of how long it lasted. Then, ten years ago, on the 50th anniversary of universal suffrage, a special Service of Commemoration to Emily Davison and the suffragettes was held at St. Mary's Parish Church, Morpeth.

On other anniversaries, one or two small plays have been staged in her honour locally. Perhaps the best known was the one-act play called, *Emily*, which was performed throughout Northumberland in 1968. Although this realistic play was written with dramatic licence, it is, nevertheless, an honest work based on extensive research. The play, by Joice Worters, of Stocksfield, was produced by Edgar Criddle, drama lecturer at Northumberland Technical College.

Mrs Worters knew both the late Dr Ethel Williams, the well-known leader of the constitutional suffragettes in Newcastle and her colleague, Miss Mabel Burnip, both of whom lived in Stocksfield after leaving Newcastle.

Emily crystallises the four attitudes towards the use of violence in the women's campaign as a whole: hostility, doubt, approval and total commitment. Miss Davison falls within the last category. But there was a strong body of Newcastle women, including Dr Williams who were non-militant.

I have talked at length with Joice Worters about the writing of her play, and she confirmed that it is based on the truth. Like the crowds turning out to see the suffragettes marching who were not friendly but 'curious'. That Emily Davison in the year of her death at the age of 40 was looking ill and tired after a three month prison sentence and a hunger strike, yet had no trace of self-pity. Emily's words, on reaching her London flat from Holloway: 'I was right glad to get away from the smell of carbolic,' ring true.

So is the description of Emily's leader, Emmeline Pankhurst after her prison confinement of hunger strikes and forced-feeding: 'Her skin all yellow and the bones of her face looking as if they're going to come through, and her eyes all bright and feverish, staring at you from great black sockets.' The dank, grim prisons conjure up a picture of great torment, the brutal infliction of force-feeding creating a hell-hole from Hogarth.

The spirit and wit of the Northumberland women is captured in Mrs Worters' lines, especially that of Mrs Mona Taylor who was one of the earliest suffragist leaders in Northumberland. Marching through Newcastle on a weekend demonstration, with crowds lining the streets one lout shouted: 'Get away home and do your washing!' Mrs Taylor was quick as a flash, 'Nowt but a slut would wash on a Saturday!'

On another demonstration, when a ruffian threw a cabbage at her, Mrs Taylor caught it and tossed it back into the crowd, 'Here,' she said, 'one of you's lost your head!'

Of Emily Davison's movement, the Women's Social and Political Union, Joice Worters said: 'In some ways, it was rather like a guerilla army and, like an army, it engendered passionate loyalties and warm comradeships.' Did Emily's great militancy speed up the cause of votes for women? 'With the wisdom of hindsight we may, perhaps contend that the tactics of the W.S.P.U. – window-smashing, assaults upon hostile politicians, hunger strikes and the like – so outraged public opinion, that they actually delayed the reform they were intended to bring about,' she said.

Though Mrs Worters added, that with the same hindsight it had to be said that Emily Davison and all the other suffragettes did a lot for the women's cause generally. 'They did a tremendous lot for women and we just accept it now, we don't even have to struggle,' she said. 'It is a pity that women like Emily Davison become forgotten heroines – they all deserve to be remembered.'

What did Joice Worters think of Emily Davison's actions today? 'I always thought that she was over the top, carried away by her religious convictions,' she said. Did she think that Emily had gone to Epsom to make the supreme sacrifice? The answer is no. 'Emily Davison was a very intelligent woman and knew that by doing that, she was not going to produce a miracle overnight and win the vote.'

Returning to Joice Worters' production, *Emily*, there is evidence here that it was the presence of the King at the Derby which attracted the attention of the suffragettes. Emily, thinking of Epsom, told her friend: 'I shan't do anything I shall be sorry for. I'll go in disguise. No flag or banners, just quiet clothes and the raven switch. Will that set your mind at rest? I'll go by train and mingle with the crowd.' In fact, whether Emily was under orders or not, she did take with her to Epsom two suffragette flags according to the Metropolitan Police list of her possessions. And there is further evidence there on how adept Emily had become at disguise and the wearing of wigs.

For a time Emily Davison did enter Northumberland folk history through a local song, or rather a sung-ditty. Old Longhorsley villagers can recall their grandparents talking about village children singing their own ditty about Emily when they played on the green. The words were never written down. One local historian thinks that the first two lines were:

'The Longhorsley lady's gone away
She's back from London another day!'

Emily herself loved to play the piano and sing. As a suffragette, two of the songs she loved were, 'Women Join Hands', written by the poet, Laurence Housman, as the 'Call to Arms' of the movement and, 'March of the Suffragettes', the popular suffrage song by Dame Ethel Smyth.

It is worth quoting a verse of 'Women Join Hands' as it captures the passionate comradeship of the fighting women:

'Heart upon heart that waited
Hands which feared to begin
Hands with hearts now mated
Hand in hand we shall win
Right is stronger than might
Higher than kingship stands
Truth with face to the light,
Women join hands, join hands!'

There were numerous other suffrage songs, some more popular than others. When the London Society for Women's Suffrage published their book, *Women's Suffrage Songs*, they inspired sympathisers to write lyrics which were set to popular tunes of the day. For example, verses of 'Shoulder to Shoulder' were set to the march, 'Men of Harlech'; 'Good Queen Bess' to the tune of 'The Vicar of Bray'; while 'Rule Britannia' was re-written by Lady Strachey with the immortal line,

'Rule, Britannia, but as you rule the waves,
Behold how all your women still are slaves!'

The same lyricist wrote the words for 'The Song for the Anti-Suffragists', which was more cutting than most and mirrored the male chauvinism of the day:

Wife:
'When we are man and wife, dear John
My very best I'll do
My wits to train, and use my brain
And grow as wise as you.'

Husband:
'No, no, my love, tho' great your charm
Your reasoning powers are small
To what I say, attention pay
And you really needn't think at all.'

Apart from fighting for the cause of suffragists, Emily Wilding Davison, throughout her life, tried to change the role of women, particularly women partners in marriage. She was always horrified to witness the plight of the young, needy mother with mouths to feed, and at her wits' end with a husband evading his responsibility to his family – or unemployed and powerless to help.

Although Emily did not have a father for the last 20 years of her life, she had a loving and devoted mother. Margaret Davison is affectionately remembered by old suffragette families in Longhorsley. She loved children and was described by one villager, as 'a real lady in the best sense of the word'. She was a generous person. 'When village children called at her corner shop to buy sweets, they always went away smiling,' said one villager. 'When the tiny hands of the children offered up a half-penny for Black Bullets, they were presented with an enormous bag-full which their little hands could hardly hold.' And when Emily Davison came home to Longhorsley to holiday and recuperate from her London exploits, she liked to entertain the village children.

Emily's affection for children is confirmed by a relative of her mother's, Mrs Dorothy Caisley of St. Mary's Field, Morpeth. She can recall stories of Emily amusing the children belonging to Grandma Caisley when she lived with her large family in the Old King's Head Yard in Morpeth. Grandma Elizabeth Caisley, had eleven children and these children called the visitor from Longhorsley, 'Auntie Emily'.

Dorothy Caisley remembers that Emily became the middle name of several of Elizabeth Caisley's daughters, and one son was named after Emily Davison's brother, Alfred Norris Davison. She said that Emily Davison still has many relations living in the Morpeth area.

Emily's mother, Margaret, was not the only member of the family to make a living baking loaves of bread and cakes. Another member of the family opened a bakery in Morpeth in what is now the Beeswing Shop.

I asked Dorothy Caisley how her own family had remembered Emily Davison. 'Emily was a very canny woman and liked to help the underdog,' she replied.

Margaret Davison's father, John Caisley, came from a mining family in Northumberland and almost certainly originated from Longhirst, near Morpeth. In the past it was thought that John Caisley came from Ulgham, though a check through the Ulgham Parish records reveals not one Caisley in the village. Janet Brown, the Ulgham local historian, confirms the total absence of Caisleys in her book of the village history. There was a drift mine at Ulgham Grange, which closed down

The village of Longhorsley of more than 70 years ago. The Rose and Thistle Inn is no more. Were these some of the village children who helped Emily Davison celebrate the news of gaining her University Degree?

The corner shop and house at Longhorsley, once the Northumberland home of Emily Davison and her mother, as it looks today. After Emily's father died, leaving less than £200 in his will, Emily's mother, Margaret, had to open a bakery here to earn a living.

in 1888. But the evidence points to Emily's grandfather coming from Longhirst, the next village. Here, the name Caisley appears in the local village records. There is mention of Robert Caisley, a miner, who married Barbara Davison (no relation to the Davisons) in 1882. Robert was the son of Thomas Caisley and a grandson of local mine-owner, William Caisley.

Margaret Caisley, Emily Davison's mother must have wondered how many children she would produce in her marriage to Charles Edward Davison, for Charles Edward already had nine to his first wife. In the event, Margaret had three, though, unhappily, she was not to spend a life-time with any of them.

Alfred Norris Davison, her first-born went out to Canada to work and died aged 48, in January 1918, in Vancouver. Ethel Henrietta, younger sister of Emily who was adored by her mother, died as an infant aged only six years. And Emily was 40 when she met her tragic death.

To add to this sad chapter of fate, Margaret Davison was only 44 years old when her husband died, though they did spend 25 years of marriage together. The large Davison family appears to have prospered, the children were all well educated and some of them entered the professions. While the Davisons settled in the South of England, Margaret, having returned to Longhorsley years before, remained in the corner shop house until her death, also in 1918, at the age of 69. Her death went unreported in local newspapers.

There is no doubt that Margaret Davison was a loving, caring person and managed the large family well. The oldest child of the first marriage, Charles Chisholm Davison, was 19 when Margaret became his step-mother, but Isobella Georgina was only 7 and John Anderson Davison only 4 years old. In between were six other step-children, though I could not discover how many were living at home at the time of the marriage. There was a close link between Isobella and her step-mother, Margaret, possibly because Isobella was very young when her own mother died and she found solace in the arms of Margaret. It is almost certain that Isobella Georgina married a Frenchman and lived at St. Malo in Normandy. Madame de Baeker of St. Malo, as the villagers recall her, was Chief Mourner at Emily's funeral with her step-mother.

Looking back to the start of the marriage with Emily's father, the records show that they were living in the South. The marriage ceremony was performed at Greenwich, though by the time Emily was born the family had moved to Blackheath.

The archives show that although the Davison family originated from Northumberland, almost without exception they preferred to live in the South. Bexhill, in Sussex and Warblington, in Hampshire, Warwick and Marylebone, were some of the places where they settled down. Charles Edward Davison, Emily's father, must also have liked the Southeast of England and London, judging by the amount of time he spent there. Not surprising, therefore, to learn that Emily Davison fell in love with London.

Although Emily engaged in a romance with the unspoiled Northumberland countryside when she stayed with her mother at Longhorsley, it was London she loved. If Longhorsley was her refuge, London was her inspiration.

Emily's poetry was not worthy of the masters, but she had the gift of expression.

'Oh, London! How I feel thy magic spell,' she once wrote.

'The centre of the universe is here! This is the hub, the very fount of life.'

What secrets Emily Wilding Davison must have stored away in the hectic life she led. She had to become a master of subterfuge in order to escape the might of the law and Scotland Yard. Often she had to lie low to escape police prying and detection. Her great interest in the theatre prompted her to learn the art of disguise, and at that she was most successful. One clue is the confusion she caused the police by presenting them with vastly different descriptions, particularly regarding the colour of her hair. I have read in different contemporary reports that her hair was coloured black, brown and even red! In fact Emily Davison had thick, golden-brown hair which was so attractive it was remarked on wherever she went. Mastering the art of disguise, she could make the quick switch into wig and working-class dress, often necessary to escape police hunting for her. Longhorsley folk recall the story that after Emily's death, a bottle of ladies' hair dye was found hidden in the chimney in her village home.

The extreme militants, like Emily Davison and Mary Leigh, could not have operated during the union's arson and bombing campaigns without resorting to disguise. There was now a strong police presence wherever they went, and a 24-hour watch was kept on the headquarters of the Women's Social and Political Union – police were after the leaders. The

Government had decided the time had come to crush the Pankhurst Movement.

The suffragettes countered that by opening up a safe-house in Camden Hill Square, London where women ex-prisoners were nursed back to health and prepared for further exploits. When detectives discovered this new hiding place – known as 'Mouse Castle' (named after the infamous 'Cat and Mouse' Act) – women from the union became 'Pimpernels in the night' in order to slip in and out of their haven.

Despite the intense activity in Emily's life at this time, she still pursued her interests outside the suffragette movement. For instance, just weeks before her death she was one of the speakers at the Workers' Educational Association meeting in the Bishopgate Institute in London. She was in good form, urging the claims of the Association in her whole-hearted way. That was probably her last public speech, in May of 1913. On the eighth day of June she had met her death. The W.E.A. newspaper, *The Highway* looking back on her association said, 'The stress of her life lay outside our limits, but with us she was happy as among friends. We are glad of it, and shall never forget her joyous presence.'

One of Emily's favourite haunts was London's Toynbee Hall, either for a cup of tea with friends or to listen to some erudite lecturer on history. Emily's zest for life, rather than a martyr's death, is much in evidence at this time. In her pocket was a ticket for a Toynbee Hall lecture on City Guilds in early June, an occasion she anticipated with relish. Fate struck her down that Epsom day. It was one lecture she would never hear.

When Emily needed to recover from her deeds she liked to travel back to Longhorsley whenever she could. In a matter of days she became rejuvenated and liked to visit Morpeth and to address public meetings. Sometimes she gave talks in the Masonic Hall which years before had been Winton House, the home of her father. The irony of appearing as a suffragette in a former family home must not have escaped her. Incidentally, when Charles Edward Davison lived there, Winton House was an imposing building in its own grounds with stables at the rear and even a tethered cow for milk!

Local suffragettes had a difficult time persuading the Morpeth electorate and the Town Council of the credibility of their cause. Twice the council rejected requests for support from the W.S.P.U. Councillor John Stafford said that if the Parliamentary 'Extension of Votes to Women' Bill was passed, 'It would breed mischief between husband and wife.' Even Lydia Becker, a pioneer of the Suffragist Movement – who had formed the first committee in England in 1867 – could make no impression on the Morpeth Town-fathers.

Even though Emily Davison had relations in high places in Morpeth – her uncle, William Davison was Mayor of Morpeth in 1879 and again in 1895 – it made no difference. Incidentally, his mill by the river Wansbeck was the first business in the town to be run on electricity, generated by water power.

Some idea of the great challenge facing local suffragettes can be seen from the parlous state of men's suffrage in the 1870s. When Thomas Burt, the first 'working man's MP' in the Morpeth Constituency was elected Liberal MP in 1874, he saw as his first job re-forming the franchise.

As leader of the Northumberland Miners' Association, he knew that many mining families in the Morpeth Division had no vote at all. Thousands living in the large villages of Bedlington, Bebside and Choppington were disfranchised. When the miners protested, they were officially told that because they lived in colliery houses and paid no rates, they were not entitled to vote. So, Thomas Burt's election address had placed 'the extension of manhood suffrage' at the top of his list of priorities. What hope had women of partaking of the 'suffrage cake' when many men were denied?

Thomas Burt's influence, and Paliamentary achievements over the years, was recognised by all Parties. Later he became Secretary of the Board of Trade. By that time he had been won over by the suffragists' cause and declared himself a supporter of the Morpeth Branch of Suffragettes.

The relationship between the Independent Labour Party and the suffragettes was not an easy one. While Keir Hardie, always a Pankhurst supporter, tried to rally the I.L.P. behind him, he often found opposition to giving women the vote within his own ranks. A good example was the reservation of Margaret Bondfield – a Wallsend MP and first woman member of the Cabinet – who clearly saw a distinction between Labour's working-class ethic and the rather middle and upper-class Party of the Women's Social and Political Union.

When challenged by a senior suffragette for her support, Miss Bondfield wished her luck and said: 'But don't let them [W.S.P.U.] come and tell me they are working for my class.'

One MP who had supported the suffragettes from his earliest days in Parliament was a deep-thinking and shrewd politician called Fenner Brockway. In later years he became one of the grandees of the Labour Party. But even he could not accept the extreme militancy of Emily Davison in her later years.

He said: 'I admired Emily Davison but could not agree with some of her attitudes. She argued that it was important to carry out acts that were both extrovert and extreme, in order to focus attention on her cause. I could not accept this theory.' Mr Brockway then broke away from the women's movement. He called Emily's arson campaign, 'an irresponsible act that did not seem in keeping with her nature.' Expressing surprise at that extreme militancy, he said he remembered her as, 'a charming and serene woman, quite attractive, feminine and sweet.' He later became Lord Brockway.

Back in Northumberland, Emily had struck up a continuing friendship with Mr and Mrs William Tennant of West Farm, Longhorsley. The Tennant farm, as well as being a hive of agricultural activity, was also a daily rendezvous for local farmers and friends. They loved to drop in for a coffee and 'a canny crack'. The hardened but generous Northumbrians used to pull Emily's leg no end, especially when she tried to sell them the unfashionable message of women's suffrage. One does not have to strain to imagine some of the ribald ripostes.

Anne Brown of Felton, in Northumberland, said that her late grandmother, Margaret Rickleton who lived in Ivy Cottage next to the farm, told the story of local farmers challenging Emily to mount an upturned tub and address them in the farmyard. One heckling farmer suggested she might be better off at home, helping her mother in the shop and darning the holes in her stockings. Emily told him that if he would display his stockings to the world, so would she. Then Emily, ever daring, lifted her skirt to show a pair of stockings perfect in every way. There were guffaws when the farmer lifted his trouser legs to show that his stockings were holed!

Mary Nesbit, who took over West Farm after the death of William and Anna Tennant, but who had lived and worked there for years before that, recalled that Emily Davison tried to convert the village into supporting women's suffrage. On summer evenings she used to stand on a barrel at the farm entrance by the roadside and sell the Cause to passers-by.

'Often farm hinds would throw bad eggs and other missiles at her, but she just carried on,' said Mary Nesbit. 'Emily used to come to the farm for a feast after starving in prison, there was always plenty of good farm food here.'

Mary, who was only a young girl when she went to work at West Farm, can recall William Tennant describing the happy times Emily Davison spent in the farm kitchen 'putting the world right' with his farmer friends. 'They all liked to talk to Emily, she was so intelligent and always had something to say,' said Miss Nesbit.

Emily used to sit on the old long-settle by the kitchen fire and carry out a non-stop conversation with all and sundry. Sometimes local preachers used to stay at the farm at weekends – that was when Emily really came into her own! Mary Nesbit remembers William Tennant saying that Emily did not set off for Epsom with the intention of making the supreme sacrifice. 'She was so full of life and eager to serve the Cause at that time; she wanted to live and carry the torch for the movement' were his words then.

She added that although the Tennants had numbers of farm horses as well as hunters in the stables, Emily never rode them. What did Mary Nesbit of Longhorsley make of Emily Davison? 'If I have one criticism of Emily's Derby Day exploit it is that it could have resulted in serious injury to other jockeys and horses, and that is not acceptable.'

But Emily never changed. When doctor and vicar had occasion to call at her mother's house, she would harangue them about universal suffrage. And when Granny Jean Jeffreys kept the Shoulder of Mutton Inn, Emily would say things to her like: 'You are very capable. You look after the inn and your family – why don't you have a vote?'

Ten years ago, on the 50th anniversary of the granting of women's suffrage, Emily and her comrades were remembered in a special Commemoration Service in Morpeth Parish Church. Although, as it transpired, it re-lit the controversy surrounding the suffragette life of Emily Davison.

In the Memorial Service the then Rector of Morpeth, the Revd Geoffrey Bateson criticised her for endangering life at Epsom. That drew the fire of a doughty little lady sitting in the congregation who later lambasted him for his remarks.

That lady was Connie Lewcock of Newcastle upon Tyne, who had been a member of the Newcastle Branch of the Suffragettes. By that time she was also a Newcastle City

Councillor, a life-time worker for the women's cause and the recipient of the O.B.E.

Revd Bateson said that actions which endangered the lives of jockeys, or even horses could not be commended by a Christian community. 'It will always be wrong to endanger the lives of human beings,' he said. Connie sitting in Church with 200 other women who had travelled from far and wide to attend, said she was 'shocked at this attitude'. After the service was over she remarked: 'I nearly stood up in the church service and protested there and then. Emily Davison is a heroine.' After half a century, feelings were still running high.

Feelings were certainly running high immediately after Emily was killed. In June alone of that year protesting women caused more than £50,000 worth of damage, a huge sum then.

That chapter of destruction included £25,000 worth of damage to a Scottish castle and £6,000 worth of damage to a southern parish church. No estimate of damage was recorded for the burning down of Gosforth Park Hall, though it must have been a huge sum.

The accounts of the W.S.P.U. showed that the union not only was wealthy, but was so well organised it could raise £15,000 at a single, Albert Hall rally. This was no 'Rag Tag and Bobtail' union of women as it was once described by the Press.

In this special year of 1988 – a triple celebration of anniversaries – 60 years since the complete vote, 70 years since the partial vote and 75 years since Emily Wilding Davison died, one may properly put the question: 'Has Miss Davison been accorded her rightful place in the history of the suffragettes?'

Many volumes have been written about Emmeline Pankhurst and her daughters. Fewer about outstanding campaigners like Emmeline Fawcett, leader of the constitutional suffragists for many years, and Lydia Becker, who formed the first suffragist committee in the country. And only one about the only woman to die for the cause and that by a novelist, albeit a good one, called Gertrude Baillie Weaver, whose pen-name was Colmore. That 61-page book was written the year Emily died.

Emily Davison was in the fore-front of the great suffragette campaign, particularly in the later, crucial years. Always a controversial figure she was, nevertheless, an innovator and inventor. Her daring in taking a leading role in the arson and bombing campaigns could not be denied. But there is no record of her having seriously injured anyone, let alone killed anyone.

A fearless suffragette, Connie Lewcock of Newcastle upon Tyne, one of Emily Davison's comrades in arms. Connie joined the suffragettes at the age of 14. At the height of the battle for women's suffrage, she drew up a plan to blow up Durham Cathedral! Connie Lewcock was 84 when this picture was taken in 1978. She died two years later.

Her indomitable courage and spirit especially in fighting brutal prison conditions and the nightmare experiences of being force-fed, set an example to other members of the Movement. As a 'soldier suffragette' she was highly decorated. She possessed the union's Scroll and Medal for Valour. The words on the Scroll, signed by Emmeline Pankhurst, tell it all:

'We, the members of the Women's Social and Political Union express our deep sense of admiration for your courage in enduring a long period of privation and solitary confinement in prison for the Votes for Women cause.'

The leader also expressed her thanks 'for the great service given to the Women's Movement'.

I noted that in the Yates Collection was a letter from W.S.P.U. Headquarters to Emily, asking her to return her medal so that one more bar could be added for carrying out yet another hunger-strike.

Emily Wilding Davison's unrelenting commitment for Emmeline and Christabel Pankhurst, are put into sharp focus with the benefit of hindsight. In that great army of women fighting 'The Holy War', she was the only one to make the supreme sacrifice on the field of battle. She pushed forward the frontiers of militancy so that Government had to act. To earn the title 'Most Militant Woman' she had to display courage of a high order. She singled herself out from the many thousands of women committed to the Cause.

At the height of the suffrage campaign, many thousands of women in Britain were involved in the battle for votes. The Pankhurst Union, alone, boasted more than 10,000 women members, of whom one tenth were activists and very militant.

In the time-span of history it is only a short period since women won the complete vote. But if Emily Davison were alive today, she would be saddened by the woefully small number of women MPs sitting in the House of Commons. Her cry would surely be for major constitutional change, and for fireworks if it did not happen! Perhaps she would be bewildered by the turn of history. The Mother of Parliaments has placed her first daughter in Downing Street, but turned her back on all but a handful of women. More women did win seats at the last general election, but the total remains pitiably small. Out of a total of 650 Members of Parliament today, only 41 are women.

One of the last pictures taken of Emily Davison. The battering she suffered from numerous prison sentences, hunger strikes and force-feeding operations is reflected on her face.

In the words of the Prime Minister, Margaret Thatcher, that is 'a great disappointment.'

In 12,000 constituency elections spanning 70 years, only 139 women became MPs. No one can deny that women in Westminster owe a great debt to the suffragettes. The march of time has proved the Emily Davison doctrine sound, though difficult to implement. That once the vote was won, women MPs must appear in great number.

Today, visitors to the Palace of Westminster will not be unaware of the Emmeline Pankhurst statue standing in Victoria Tower gardens. Perhaps if one more statue stood in the shadow of Parliament it might manage a wry smile. But the head of this suffragette would be to one side, asking the question: 'Where are the women?' And what would Emily Davison say to selection committee women who preferred men to women as Parliamentary candidates? Or to the hierarchy of the main Parties who place many women in unwinnable seats? Or, perhaps more to the point, what action would Miss Davison be taking now?

We shall never know. But we do know that she deserves to join the Roll of Honour bearing illustrious names of 'Women of the North'. Women like Josephine Butler, liberator of women, Emily Davies, leading educationalist, and Ellen Wilkinson, Jarrow marcher and Government Minister.

Emily Wilding Davison was the maverick of the suffragette movement, whose great courage inspired hundreds of women around her. She set fire to that turbulent era, the great war fought over Women's Suffrage.

And if her extreme form of militancy did not win the battle in her life-time, it blazed forth the message for women's rights and equality throughout the nation.

Five years after her violent death – which included four years of a World War – the first women won the vote.

BIBLIOGRAPHY AND ACKNOWLEDGEMENTS

The Life of Emily Davison An Outline by Gertrude Colmore (The Woman's Press, Imprint of the Women's Social and Political Union).

Votes for Women by Roger Fulford (Faber and Faber Ltd.)

Rapiers and Battleaxes by Josephine Kamm (George Allen and Unwin Ltd.)

Memories of a Militant by Annie Kenney (Edward Arnold & Co)

A Northumbrian Remembers by Nancy Ridley (Robert Hale).

Emily by Joice Worters (One-Act Play produced by Edgar Criddle, Northumberland Technical College. Published by J. & J. S. MacKay, Morpeth.)

Those Misguided Women (A short history of the Tynedale Campaign by Janet Earnshaw, Doreen Godson, Pat Hare, Margaret Hinchcliffe, Carol Mason, Liz Nesbit, Jean Spry, Ann Wilkinson, Brigit Wren and Anna Rossiter.)

Rose Lamartine Yates Collection (The Fawcett Library at the City of London Polytechnic).

The Museum of London

Suffragettes in the North-East by David Neville (A Paper for the North-East Labour History Society).

A Howky Gan Te Parliement, Thomas Burt MP (Northumberland County Library Service. First edition by William Strachan, Headmaster, Preston Grange County Primary).

The Suffragette (Editions various)

Suffragette Fellowship Newsletter

Newcastle Chronicle and Journal Ltd.

Morpeth Herald

Hexham Courant

News Post, Blyth

Illustrated Chronicle

The Sunday Times

The *Daily Herald*

Department of the Environment Press Office

Hansard, Official Parliamentary Record

Daily Telegraph

Women's Suffrage Songs, London Society for Women's Suffrage

10 Downing Street Press Office

Daily Mirror

Acknowledgements

Vera Baird, London (Late of Northumberland)
Roland Bibby, Morpeth Local Historian
Janet Brown (Author of *Ulgham*, a village history)
Canon Terence Oliver, Longhorsley
Margaret Oliver, Longhorsley Local Historian
Meg Burdon, Morpeth County Library
Anne Brown, Felton
Dorothy Caisley, Morpeth
Catherine Ireland and David Doughan (Fawcett Library)
Deborah Jeffreys, Longhorsley
Margaret Johnstone, Morpeth
Mary Nesbit, Longhorsley
Robert Robson, Longframlington
Winnie Stobbart, late of Longhorsley
Sylvia Stokoe, Morpeth Chantry Local Museum
Isobel Smail, Morpeth Antiquarian Society
Alec Tweddle, Morpeth Local Historian
BBC Hulton Picture Library
Kaspar Yeeles, Morpeth
Tom Breckons
Bill Wallace, Appleby's Book Shop Morpeth
Association of Northumberland Local History Societies
Northumberland County Records Office
Northumberland County Council Press Office
Castle Morpeth Borough Council
Morpeth Parish Council
Newcastle upon Tyne City Library (Local History Section)
Gosforth Public Library